*The School Library*

# The School Library

RALPH E. ELLSWORTH

*Director of Libraries*
*Professor of Bibliography*
*University of Colorado*

The Center for Applied Research in Education, Inc.
*New York*

LIBRARY OF CONGRESS
CATALOG CARD NO.: 65-15520

PRINTED IN THE UNITED STATES OF AMERICA

# *Foreword*

To those of us whose profession is both education and librarianship, the school library has long foreshadowed coming events in both the school and the library.

In the pages you are about to read, you will be aroused by a new breakthrough. Ralph Ellsworth has caught the vision of a school that is essentially a library, and of a library that is fundamentally a school. This was the dream that Commissioner William Torrey Harris had a half-century ago. This is now the emerging reality sketched in a design for the library-centered school.

Such a library-centered school, when it comes, will most certainly be as educationally committed to independent learning and self-teaching as Dr. Ellsworth suggests. In such an environment, the school library can at last approach the role that some visionaries have described in the wilderness for so long. In this role, the school library will function as the teacher of that neglected half of knowledge—"the knowledge of where to find it"—and as the interdisciplinary synthesizer which establishes, as Dr. Ellsworth puts it: "interrelations among various fields of knowledge."

In this library there will be a carefully selected representation of all the school media that communicate the record of man's noblest thoughts and deeds. Dr. Ellsworth calls these media *carriers,* and he conceives them, basically, as printed matter. But he also understands the place of other formats, from television to teaching machines, and the unity concept of materials that has for two decades occupied the Florida schools in linking audiovisualists and librarians in a common cause.

The housing of school library materials is, in many ways, one of the most frustrating of all architectural challenges. Part of the inadequacy of the past resulted from the great variety of formats found in our nation's school libraries, even greater than that found in other kinds of libraries. Another cause is the unfulfilled potential of the library in the school. Only a librarian with Dr. Ellsworth's creativity in library architecture could possibly cope with these challenges. I daresay school librarianship and school architecture will be awakened to new opportunities by Chapter VI.

But even more fundamental to the library-centered school than materials or housing is the concept of the librarian-teacher. Dr. Ellsworth, if I read him right, is predicting a new breed of school personnel—a cross between the present professional librarian and the classroom teacher. If that comes about, look for the breakthrough in both secondary and elementary education that critics of our nation's schools have long sought.

And when that breakthrough comes, Dr. Ellsworth's volume will be one of the bibles of the new American education.

LOUIS SHORES
*Florida State University*

# The School Library

## Ralph Ellsworth

Dr. Ellsworth's treatment of the school library is concerned primarily with library service in the secondary school, although much of what he recommends is applicable also to the elementary school. The author's ideas about effective library service in the high school are in many instances drawn from the experience of colleges and universities.

The book departs somewhat from the usual pattern found in other volumes of the Library of Education. The emphasis here is distinctly *not* on a descriptive account of the present situation in school libraries. Dr. Ellsworth finds the library service so deplorably inadequate in the typical American high school that he believes a fresh, new start is required. He calls for sweeping, almost breathtaking redirection and innovation, while he describes, not what is, but what ought to be. He urges a revitalization of the whole concept of the use of the library as an educational resource. His suggestions for the kinds of equipment needed, for the size of the book collection, and for the nature of the service by the librarian are far beyond current practices in all but a few of those schools that are generally recognized as superior.

The high goals the author sets are not unattainable. They represent the direction toward which better high schools are moving rapidly. With current pressures to improve standards of achievement by high school pupils, it may not be long before communities in every state will be introducing the kind of facilities for library service that Dr. Ellsworth recommends.

The author is no armchair theorist on library matters. He has been in the profession of librarianship for a long time. He has had unusual opportunities to visit schools widely throughout the country and to observe their libraries critically. He has recently completed a significant study of school library services for the Educational Facilities Laboratories of the Ford Foundation.

The book on *The School Library* finds its place in the Library of Education alongside other volumes that treat the personnel and material resources related to the school environment. The librarian is just a specialized teacher, and so the discussion of her preparation and personality is parallel to that of other school personnel found in *The Teacher and Learning, The School Counsellor,* and *The Profession of Teaching.* With respect to the material aspects of the school library, the discussion is somewhat parallel to that in the volume, *Audiovisual Instruction.*

JOHN DALE RUSSELL
*Content Editor*

# Contents

# CHAPTER I

# Background Factors

## Introduction

The organization and nature of this volume will necessarily differ somewhat from that of the others in the Library of Education because it deals with a subject about which one might say that its past lies in the future. So little attention was given to school libraries prior to the 1960's, and the nature of that which was given was so uncritical and unsophisticated, that there is no solid record of research and scholarship upon which to base an analysis. At best, one is forced to speculate on background factors and to project, from current developments, lines of future development.

Reference will frequently be made to those developments in the college library field which began in the mid-1930's, because college librarians began at that time to face up to the problems and opportunities that elementary and secondary school librarians were ready to meet in the 1960's. Although, naturally, the various levels of education differ from one another in many respects, the tremendous improvements in teaching methods made by the elementary and secondary schools since World War II have resulted in the preparation of high school students who are, in many respects, capable of doing college-level work. By the same token, the college-level experience with a broad concept of the honors program in the 1960's was found to be applicable to many students in the secondary schools. During this time, directors of libraries in universities which maintained experimental or laboratory secondary schools found that library programs that proved effective for the college student were equally valuable for the high school student. Because much experimentation with the library as a teaching instrument was conducted at the college level, and because the results promise to be relevant for high school libraries, this volume will draw heavily from the college-level experiments.

In the course of writing a report on the architectural aspects of the school library in 1963,[1] the authors found no school libraries in existence in the United States that met the criteria they considered essential, although a few (such as the University of Chicago Laboratory High School, the South Cheyenne High School near Colorado Springs, Colorado, and the West Leydon, Illinois, High School) were outstanding in comparison with the rest. They could find no existing school library good enough to serve as an architectural model for the future. In fact, they found no public secondary school libraries large enough to be housed in a separate building. In England, on the other hand, several of the boarding schools—Aldenham, Bedaler, and Sidborgh, for example—had separate library buildings.[2]

When the Educational Facilities Laboratories report was written in 1963, there were over ten million American students attending schools that had no library at all, and the majority of the existing school libraries were appallingly inadequate. In 1946 a majority of the entering freshmen at the State University of Iowa were found by the author (with the help of the Registrar at that University) to have come from high schools that had no libraries. There were, at that time, fewer than a dozen high schools in the state of Iowa that had libraries worthy of the name.

Dozens of books and hundreds of journal articles have been written on the subject of school libraries (see articles listed under appropriate headings in the various volumes of *Library Literature*)[3] but most of these were based on a concept of the library that did not meet the needs of the schools in the 1950's.[4] In fact, until 1960, when Francis Henne's "Toward Excellence"[5] and the American Library Association's *Standards for School Library Programs*[6] were published, and 1962, when the Knapp School Libraries project was put into operation, there was very little literature that was helpful except as background material.

[1] Ralph E. Ellsworth and Hobart Wagener, *The School Library* (New York: Educational Facilities Laboratory, Inc., 1963).

[2] Anthony Thompson, *Library Buildings of Britain and Europe* (London: Butterworth & Co. [Publishers], Ltd., 1963), p. 213ff.

[3] *Library Literature,* ed. Dorothy Cole (New York: H. W. Wilson Co., 1921+).

[4] Nora E. Beust, *School Library Standards, 1954.* U.S. Office of Education Bulletin No. 15 (Washington, D.C.: USGPO, 1954).

[5] Francis Henne, "Toward Excellence," *Library Quarterly* (January 1960), 75–90.

[6] American Association of School Libraries, *Standards for School Library Programs* (Chicago: American Library Association, 1960).

Emphasis in this volume will therefore be placed on ideas and developments that are shaping the future of school libraries, rather than on the older practices that were characteristic of school libraries prior to World War II.

Theory will be emphasized because it is essential to an understanding of why the older school libraries were inadequate and why the new concepts have evolved. The discussion will necessarily range widely in order to present all the elements that formed the past record and that constitute the foundation for the future. Background is examined, not for its own sake, but for the help it offers in establishing models for the future. The validity of the presentation will be measured, in part, by how well it describes developments of the last half of the twentieth century.

### The Desire for Improvement

Interest in improving the quality of school library service began to spread in the 1960's. It could be seen in the American Association of School Libraries' publication, *Standards for School Library Programs,* in the imaginative Knapp School Library project, and in the interest of school administrators and architects revealed in the hundreds of new school buildings constructed after World War II. The many new publications on school planning by Educational Facilities Laboratories, Inc., were also eloquent testimony to the widespread interest in libraries.

But these developments raised a question: Why had the American public schools been able to get along for a century without good school libraries and without librarians? The question is relevant because if the status, use, and operation of a school library reflect accurately the nature and quality of the instructional program, an analysis of the changes in the school library over a period of years should reveal much about the school it serves. The question is important also because the widespread desire for improved library service in the 1960's could not be satisfied unless the causes for dissatisfaction with past performance were understood. If a library bears an organic relationship to the instructional program of the school, then it follows that improvement of the library depends on improvement of the program.

The evidence of this organic relationship at the college level has been documented,[7] but whether the same relationship holds for the secondary level will not be demonstrated until a substantial number of adequate school libraries have had a chance to operate in schools in which the instructional program permits proper use of the library.

In the older secondary schools, with libraries typical of the pre-1960 years, one could be fairly certain that the teaching methods used were limited to a formal "cell-and-bell," highly organized combination of classroom-presentation-and-textbook-study pattern. The student's day was filled with five or six classroom periods and only one free hour for study—a full day. The school probably contained a study hall which *was* the library, or at least the main part of it. The school library probably had fewer than a thousand good book titles in it and it was not open for use in the late afternoon, during the evening, or on weekends. There was a wide and unbridged operational and psychological gap between the librarian and the faculty. The school administrators were aware that there was something wrong with the library, but they attributed the situation to the librarian's lack of imagination, enlightenment, or ability. The librarians, in turn, placed the blame on conditions imposed by the school administrators. It did not occur to either group that the causes were more fundamental.

In the long run, the nature of the library program and the intent of the school administrator determine the kind of librarian that will be attracted to a specific library. To put it another way, it is usually true that the nature of the people selected to do a job is determined by the employer's image of the task. A strong and able librarian can sometimes improve a mediocre library situation, but unless she can change the philosophy of education and the teaching procedures and schedules which prevail in the school, her impact will not be noticeable. A proper understanding of who is responsible for the quality of school library service will not be reached until it is understood that the status, use, and operation of a school library are the result of the nature and character of the total instructional program of the school.

---

[7] Harvie Branscomb, *Teaching with Books* (Chicago: American Library Association, 1931), and Patricia Knapp, "The Monteith Experiment," *College and Research Libraries* (July 1961), 257–58.

## Preconditions

Although there probably has never been a time since 1800 when all the public schools of the country followed only one philosophy of education or one method of teaching, it would be safe to say that in the nineteenth century—or even in the first quarter of the twentieth century, the public schools assumed that it was their major responsibility to teach the mastery of the principal cultural tools: reading, writing, and arithmetic—the 3 R's, as they were called. The rigors of Latin declensions were believed to train not only the mind but the man as well. Strength of character was held to be the natural by-product of arduous mental labor.[8] The ability to orate and to use literary quotations or allusions were considered essential skills for anyone who expected to take part in ordinary social life. The person who didn't know his classics would be unable to understand the articles and stories in the popular magazines. The ability to do simple arithmetic problems in one's head was essential in the preadding-machine days.

In the nineteenth century, the lessons of classical history seemed applicable to most of the major problems that confronted Americans. Because government, except in a few large cities, was simple, elementary, and not a major problem for the individual, the schools did not need to spend much time preparing students for citizenship —a simple course in civics provided the necessary information on local, state, and federal governments. Except for the problem of slavery, the moral issues facing the citizen were largely related to personal behavior, for which the churches provided the necessary guidance. The differences people had with one another were local and uncomplicated; most could be solved face to face, without the necessary intervention of a complex government. The individual was more conscious of his areas of personal freedom than of the areas of restriction imposed by state, federal, or international authority.

Entrance to the professions could be casual. One could become a lawyer by "reading for the law."

It was not necessary for the school to concern itself with matters

---

[8] An unidentified quotation in the author's files. It is used because it expresses well one kind of classical point of view of the concept of discipline in education.

of theories of aesthetics. Literary style was fairly straightforward and easily comprehended; most American art was representational; most of the music that the average man (outside the largest cities, at least) had a chance to hear was simple and could be appreciated without special preparation.

Most of the solutions to the problems arising out of daily life—from rearing a child to treating a horse for colic or greasing a buggy axle—were known to adults and could be learned by youth "on the job," so to speak. Every boy learned how to take apart his coaster wagon or bicycle and to put it back together again. Driver-training courses were hardly necessary.

Nor was the nineteenth-century school torn in two over the dilemma of vocational training versus academic preparation. Few graduated from the secondary school and even fewer went on to college. Private schools existed for those children whose parents could afford to send them to college. The state university played a minor role.

In the nineteenth century, therefore, the secondary school did not need large reservoirs of information (libraries) to carry out their relatively simple assignments. The textbooks could present the necessary factual information and could, at the end of each chapter, ask the essential questions. Society knew the relevant questions—and the answers as well. The large, multivolumed anthology of the great literary masterpieces, such as the *Library of the World's Best Literature* (1896), provided the texts of the classical writings and the sources from which literary quotations could be learned. The *Encyclopedia Britannica* provided scholarly treatments (at least through the Eleventh Edition) of most of the questions a student in a high school would be asking. Cheap paperbacks of most of the better-known literary masterpieces were available—and because the schools made no attempt to teach the works of minor writers, the unavailability of their works was not a serious matter.

Although science made great strides in the nineteenth century, the secondary schools were not much affected by it in a manner that bore any implications for the school library. Science was taught, but as a series of facts rather than as a method of arriving at truth (except in very limited areas of knowledge). Evidence, or proof, for the problems with which the school dealt consisted largely of quotations from history, classical literature, or the Bible. A mass of relevant statements from great men constituted the basis for proof. Only in the limited areas of the biological or geological sciences were the schools able to use problems whose solutions rested on a foundation of facts that could be tested empirically, or scientifically. Few, if any, secondary schools had science laboratories.

Thus the amount of "evidence" that seemed to be needed in the schools could be contained in a small number of books or anthologies. There was little need for librarians to organize large collections of books, journals, documents, or pamphlets, or to help students learn how to extract information from a wide variety of sources. Textbooks took care of the matter.

Nor did the teaching methods of the nineteenth century require large reference collections in the high school libraries. At the college level, methods implied by the phrase *Mark Hopkins on one end of a log and a student on the other* left no place for the library or the laboratory. Necessary evidence could be communicated orally or found in the classics.

Close study of the textbooks provided sufficient information to satisfy the needs of the class recitations. Preparations for papers, debates, or oratorical contests relied heavily on marshalling relevant quotations from the great writers, so about all a school library needed was a few sets of *Selections from . . . ,* a Bible, a dictionary, an atlas, and a few miscellaneous reference books.

The school library was not a problem that commanded the attention of professors of education during the nineteenth century or the first third of the twentieth.[9] But the character of the country began to change, both before and after the turn of the century, as a result of many developments—the closing of the frontier; the building of transcontinental railroads; the invention of the automobile, the telephone, the telegraph, the phonograph, and the motion picture; and the introduction of techniques of mass production, not to mention the impact of the new science. With these changes, the scope of the problems society expected the schools to deal with began to

---

[9] To test this generalization, the author examined the tables of contents and indexes of the education books in the University of Colorado Library written during that period. There were no references to *school libraries* or *librarians* and only occasionally did the word *book* appear. Admittedly, this proves only that writers of textbooks on secondary education did not write about libraries, but one may assume that they would have done so if the library had been an important problem in the school. It wasn't.

expand rapidly. Mastery of the disciplines of the nineteenth century was not sufficient to equip students to take their part in the adult life of the early twentieth century.[10]

## The Forces of Change

Near the turn of the century, schoolmen began to think about teaching in a new way—a way that had a pronounced effect on school libraries. This change in attitude came about through the influence of two forces: the new psychology, and John Dewey.

Although it is axiomatic that the best teachers of all time have been as much interested in their students as in the subjects they taught or the teaching methods they used, the new psychology of learning[11] opened up so many new ways of thinking about the student as a learner that the teachers could hardly avoid concentrating on this new subject—the child—and on the possibilities of new teaching methods based on the new psychology. The idea that better results in the classroom could be achieved by studying teaching methods scientifically was an exciting one. Any teacher worthy of the name could hardly avoid being caught up in the enthusiasm and optimism that permeated the normal schools, teachers colleges, and university departments of education and psychology in the first half of the twentieth century. Psychological experiments on learning and on teaching methods were conducted, new journals were founded, and it seemed that a new science of teaching—one that could be taught to future teachers—was being created. This enthusiasm became translated into sequences of courses constituting a major in education, into graduate programs leading to the master's and doctoral degrees, into requirements for teaching backed by state certification laws (replacing earlier types of teacher preparation that stressed only the acquisition of knowledge of the subject matter to be taught). These changes are the foundation of all modern developments in American education.

This force alone would probably have had little influence on the development of school libraries; but, coupled with the second force

---

10 Francis Chase and Harold A. Anderson, *High Schools in a New Era* (Chicago: The University of Chicago Press, 1958), and Francis Chase, "America Evaluates its Schools," *Library Quarterly* (1960), 4.

11 William James, *Talks to Teachers* (New York: Holt, Rinehart & Winston, Inc., 1905).

—John Dewey's concept of interest and effort in education[12]—the effect was explosive.

The impact of John Dewey, and of his followers, interpreters, and misinterpreters, on modern education needs no detailed explanation here. His effect on school libraries, though indirect and possibly unintentional, marked the dividing line between the old concept of a library and the new. Dewey placed his stamp of approval on the idea of bringing into the teaching process, as teaching materials, the many new developments and problems in modern society. Or, to put the matter more specifically, it became inevitable that schoolmen contemplating the implications of Dewey's interpretation of the use of pupil interest in learning should want to use the problems of contemporary life as tools for feeding and stimulating interest in learning. This meant that the schools had to find and organize the factual information on current phenomena, and this meant that they had to have libraries. Just as the new interest in science brought to light a new way of thinking and of arriving at the truth, so Dewey's concept created the realization that the phenomena of contemporary society provided better teaching materials than did the selections from the old masters. The multivolume anthology became a multithousand volume school library. The index volume, in a manner of speaking, was transformed into the librarian.

The American public takes for granted the propriety of infusing the public secondary school with the problems faced by contemporary society. The assumption is that it is better to illustrate the principles being taught by problems that are real to the students rather than by illustrations from remote times and places. In fact, some groups, like the Council on Basic Education, feel that the schools have gone too far and have let local and contemporary illustrations dominate the principles and substitute for disciplines.

The public often becomes uneasy when the schools use, as teaching materials, problems that represent radical departures from educational traditions. This is particularly true when contemporary literature is used to help students understand a new point of view. For example, Salinger's *Catcher in the Rye* has been used in literature and social studies classes, and was therefore placed in the secondary school library, because it carries to high school students a

---

[12] John Dewey, *Interest and Effort in Education* (Boston: Houghton Mifflin Company, 1913).

message they seemed to need and to understand, even though some adults find the book shocking or crude. In the nineteenth-century library, such books would not have been present: they were not considered relevant, for contemporary literature was not taught. The problems that serious writers used as the basis for their art were not appropriate for the high school curriculum. The Horatio Alger or Oliver Topic books and the dime novels were not placed in the school libraries, but they were nevertheless read widely by the young people. It was from such books that most American children first learned of the heartaches of the immigrant child, or of the idealism of the American Dream—not as theory but as the emotional struggles of vivid characters in novels.

So, as the problems of early twentieth-century America began to find a place in the curriculum of the public school, replacing the classical literary and historical subjects, the school libraries began to include books concerned with banks and business, tariffs, wars, slums, crime, advertising, automobiles, airplanes, labor unions, robber-barons, main street, cigarettes, and sex. The books representing the classical literary heritage gathered dust on the shelves. The study of modern languages flourished, while the study of Greek and Latin declined. The thundering of Paul Shorey, the last of the great eloquent spokesmen for the classics in the 1920's, was listened to only by those whose views now had become a minority voice in public education.

# CHAPTER II

# Negative Forces

Although the intellectual power generated by the new psychology and Dewey's concepts should have caused the school libraries to flourish, something happened between the two world wars that stunted their growth. It is strange indeed that this should have happened at the very time that college and university libraries were passing through a most remarkable period of growth and use, and at a time when the public schools themselves were growing in size and scope and the departments of education in colleges and universities were making their influence felt. No one has as yet sorted out, in proper order of importance, all the factors that were responsible for this hiatus.

## The School Administrator

Society's forcing of responsibility on the American public schools for teaching a multitude of new subjects—plus requiring them to teach new skills, attitudes, and habits that earlier generations had learned in the home—had the effect of enlarging and complicating the operations of the schools to such an extent that the administrative tasks became too numerous and complicated to be handled by already overburdened teachers. Administration became a full-time endeavor and, thus, a basically new element in the school.

The pressures of the times were such that administrators—like lawyers, doctors, ministers, and teachers—could not take the time to learn their craft on the job. The learning process could be shortened and improved by professional study and instruction. Prospective administrators began to concentrate their graduate studies in educational administration, not in the traditional subject disciplines. To meet their needs, the colleges and universities offered extensive programs in administration. A gap began to form between administration and the traditional fields of learning. This situation was also aggravated by the fact that school administration attracted many re-

11

cruits, not among teachers of the traditional subjects, but among members of athletic coaching staffs and teachers of vocational and commercial subjects. Thus the gap between administration and traditional learning was widened.

This problem was discussed with heat and bitterness in the 1950's and the 1960's and the lines of debate were hard and sharp. Robert M. Hutchins, Arthur Bestor's *The Educational Wastelands*[1] and *The Restoration of Learning*,[2] Admiral Rickover, and the Council of Basic Education were the most articulate spokesmen for traditional learning. The administrators' arguments continued to be stated in their journals. Arthur Mayers' *The Schools*[3] and the various writings of James Conant and Paul Woodring attempted to find a middle ground.

The nature of this gap has been well stated by Dr. N. B. Burbank, President of the American Association of School Administrators in 1962, in an interview published in his hometown newspaper:

> No longer is it enough to have had some courses in education and administration, and a subject major and minor. He (the school administrator) finds himself frequently in deep water if he doesn't have a fair degree of familiarity with such cognate fields as economics, sociology, anthropology, philosophy, and political science. In other words, he needs a broad cultural preparation in liberal arts as well as thorough training in the fields of educational administration.[4]

Unfortunately for the debate, few viewed the problem as it really was: a situation in which an administrator, no matter what his educational and personal background, found himself in the midst of a communitywide disagreement over the fundamental purpose of the school—a situation in which the administrator's time had to be spent on budgets, bond issues, buildings, community factions, Supreme Court decisions, personnel policies, public relations, and many other such worrisome matters that put the quiet, scholarly life of the old headmaster almost completely out of reach. This dilemma was also well stated by Burbank:

---

[1] Arthur Bestor, *The Educational Wastelands* (Urbana: University of Illinois Press, 1953).

[2] Arthur Bestor, *The Restoration of Learning* (New York: Alfred A. Knopf, Inc., 1955).

[3] Arthur Mayers, *The Schools* (New York: Harper & Row, Publishers, 1961).

[4] N. B. Burbank, interviewed by the Boulder, Colorado, *Daily Camera,* May 14, 1962.

An overriding problem, one which may well outstrip all others in urgency, is found in the tensions which have come in recent years to be an integral part of your daily life and mine. The larger our district becomes, the more our enrollment grows, the more we find ourselves embroiled in tension-producing activities. More and more prized is the ability to go home and relax in the evening and get a good night's sleep. Too few of us can still do this—most of us are lucky if we get away for two or three weeks in the summer. The complexities of our responsibilities today are indeed far reaching.[5]

Regardless of the reasons for the existence of the problem, the fact is that the school administrators of the post-World War I years have been responsible for school systems in which school libraries have been characterized by their absence—or, when present, by their meagerness and low quality. One does not find in the writings of these administrators much real concern over this lack. The administrators may or may not be reflecting the wishes of the community or the teaching staffs. Nevertheless, the responsibility is theirs.

## The Student's Workday

There have been few, if any, secondary schools in modern times in which students were left on their own responsibility each day for many hours of undirected reading or study. In the post-World War I school, as the range of subjects widened, the student day was divided into five or six scheduled class periods, with no—or at most one—free study period. Early mornings or later afternoons were filled with musical, athletic, or other nonacademic activities. Evenings were for homework.

The pace and timing of this kind of day did not foster the forming of reading habits such as the individual needs for adult life or for college. The library was a place to which the pupil might go to find specific information, but he had to ask permission to go there. It was not a place in which he might spend several hours in unscheduled reading. (The author well remembers his own experience in the West Waterloo, Iowa, high school, where one had to have at least a B average before he could go to the school library.)

---

[5] *Ibid.*

## The School Library

The school libraries of the post-World War I period seldom provided seating for more than 1–5 per cent of the student body. They were usually uninviting places with uncomfortable furniture, no privacy, and almost none of the graces one expects to find in the place where he spends his precious learning hours.

## The Study Hall-Library Concept

As late as the 1960's, most school libraries were little more than study halls, to which the students were sent for an hour a day to study their textbooks under the close supervision of the school librarian or of a teacher assigned to relieve the school librarian. This procedure presumably provided an opportunity for students to be exposed to the books and magazines in the library. The classroom teachers thus gained a little free time during the day and the school librarian had an opportunity to provide reading counseling for the students.

That was the theory, but in practice the idea worked out quite differently.[6] Students resented the enforced study period and rebelled against it. This attitude was exhibited by the dozens of students seen personally by the author and by the hundreds reported on by the librarians who supervised them.[7]

The school librarian (or the classroom teacher who came in to relieve her) spent her time trying to make the students behave and to keep some kind of order in the room. Few students tried to use the library as a reference source. Placing the study hall in the library had little or no effect on the students' attitude toward study. The library environment itself had no effect in inducing library use. The serious students were so loaded with textbook assignments in their study-hall periods that they had no time to use library books. And the nonserious students were killing time and trying to enjoy themselves. The librarian had little opportunity to do any reading counseling or to work with the faculty on ways and means of enriching the materials for the teaching program.

---

[6] Lucille Fargo, *The Library in the School* (Chicago: American Library Association, 1947).

[7] *Library Literature,* under heading *Study hall.*

The study hall-library combination failed, and now is seldom recommended in the textbooks on school administration. While it lasted, it wrecked the enthusiasm, high hopes, and plans of many good young school librarians, and the image of school librarianship it created made recruiting very difficult. In spite of the fact that the plan has been recognized as a failure, it was still in common use in many high schools in the early 1960's.

### The School Librarian

Early in the 1960's the American Association of School Libraries recognized that something drastic needed to be done to raise the quality of school library service and to bring a larger number of well-qualified librarians into the field. To accomplish this, the Association organized a School Library Development project which engaged in many useful activities, including the publishing of worthwhile articles. The Association also established the Knapp Foundation School Library Project with a $1.3 million grant to support a five-year plan "to demonstrate the educational value of a full program of school library services."

In spite of the self-criticism among school librarians, revealed in the hundreds of journal articles they wrote about themselves and their work each year, the fact that the Knapp Project could be activated rapidly is adequate testimony that there were large numbers of imaginative, well-prepared, and personable school librarians in the field. Why, then, was progress so late in coming? Based on what this author learned from fourteen years as Supervisor of the State University of Iowa Laboratory School libraries, from visiting hundreds of school libraries, from careful reading of the literature in the field, from work with architects and school administrators on several school library projects, from conversations with dozens of schoolmen, and from the experience gained in preparing the manuscript for *The School Library* for Educational Facilities Laboratories, Inc., he feels safe in concluding that the major responsibility for poor school library service lies not with the school librarians as such but with *all* the factors that are discussed in this chapter. Even if a majority of practicing school librarians were perfect, the pattern of library service could not be changed much. Only by eliminating the weak element in each factor can a better result be obtained. The salaries and working conditions that have been offered to school librarians have not been sufficiently attractive to draw enough of the right kind of men and women into the profession.

## The Schoolteacher

One of the favorite fantasies of school librarians involves working in a school in which each teacher has the ability, the personality, the patience, the tools, and the time to stimulate in each of her pupils a desire for learning so intense that they will break down the doors of the library to get at the books. Although the school teaching staffs are not full of Americanized versions of Mr. Chips, most schools have a few teachers that manage, in one way or another, to capture the imagination of some of their pupils and to stimulate their interest in reading. That this happens at all is a tribute to the strength of the American secondary schools. The author's grateful memory of the North Des Moines, Iowa, high school teachers, whose words of encouragement gave him courage to tackle college, seems not too unusual.

Again, one may judge the nature of the situation by considering the dramatic actions that are taken to improve it. The efforts of the Fund for the Advancement of Education since 1950 to find ways of freeing teachers from all the boring details that detract from their effectiveness stand as one bit of evidence of the fact that improvements are needed.

Enough is known about the essential role of the teacher in stimulating reading to permit the conclusion that, if school library service is to be improved, more teachers will have to be found who know how to stimulate the desire to learn among pupils. Then these teachers and their pupils will have to be given the working conditions necessary for the fulfillment of their intentions and abilities.

In the 1950's and early 1960's, the possible and the probable seemed separated by a very wide gap. The fact needs to be made clear that the kind of education teachers were getting as late as the 1960's, even at the graduate level, may have been useful in giving them the knowledge they needed but it was most inadequate in teaching them the books that contained the knowledge.

And if the role of the teacher as a stimulator of reading was to be improved, society had to find tangible ways of providing teachers with income, status, and opportunity for self-improvement, so that a lifetime devoted to teaching would earn for a teacher the distinction of being a person of learning.

## The School Library as
## a Place for Reading

As stated earlier, when the Educational Facilities Laboratories report on the school library was written,[8] the authors could find no school libraries that offered the physical environment they felt was essential. Most existing school libraries consisted of a rectangular room with a few rows of tables down the center, bookcases against the walls, and a supervising librarian's charging desk in the middle of the room or near the door. Sometimes a small seminar room was provided and, occasionally a small office for the librarian and an even smaller workroom for consultation with teachers. Almost never were adequate provisions made for handling nonbook types of learning materials. Seldom were any provisions made for comfort and privacy—no lounge-type furniture, few reading-room carrels, few carpeted areas, and no facilities recognizing the very special physical needs of readers at the high school age. The Educational Facilities Laboratories report was written to show what could be done. Wagener's prototype designs[9] were presented to stimulate thinking on these matters. The Kornberg carrel[10] provided a new design for the kind of learning center the learning technology of the 1960's would appear to make possible.

The idea that physical environment can make a contribution to the learning process is nothing new. Until the 1960's, however, the American schools had seldom been allowed to use the talents of imaginative architects in building schools that provided many architectural graces. Intense resistance against the luxury of these buildings was not easily overcome. Some of the fine college and university libraries of the period—Bennington College, Colorado College, Douglass College, Beaver College, Mount St. Scholastica College,

---

[8] Ralph E. Ellsworth and Hobart Wagener, *The School Library* (New York: Educational Facilities Laboratory, Inc., 1963).

[9] *Ibid.*, pp. 56–72, 97ff.

[10] Educational Facilities Laboratories, Inc., *Study Carrels—Designs for Independent Study Space* (Stanford: The School Planning Laboratory, Stanford University, 1963).

Grinnell College, Georgia Institute of Technology, Washington University, the University of Michigan undergraduate library, Miami University, to mention only a few—gave architects a precedent for attempting similar results in the public schools. Early results suggest the worthiness of the attempt. Compare the typical school library on page 15 of the Educational Facilities Laboratories report with the other pictures in the report to see what can be done.

Too frequently the high school library has been hidden away in a part of the building where the students have to make an extra effort to use it. Examples of poorly located libraries can be found everywhere. A typical example would be the Naperville, Illinois, High School before Superintendent Harry Koss enlarged the building and provided a better location.

## The Intellectual Tone
## of the American School System

This question of the intellectual tone of the American school system has been so infused with emotion and prejudice that a sensible and objective discussion of it is nearly impossible. Rickover, in his *Education and Freedom*,[11] spoke for one element. Some of the country's intellectuals, rightly or wrongly, shared Rickover's opinion that the public school had become so involved with what they considered irrelevancies that they could see no hope for the future intellectual life of the nation.

Others, and it would appear that they represented the predominant view, readily admitted the weaknesses in the school system but, instead of spending their time looking for culprits, settled down to improve conditions. In this group should be included the national associations of the teachers of biology, chemistry, mathematics, and physics.[12] The National Council of the Teachers of English has also worked intelligently at the problem.

But, regardless of how one assesses the conditions, there is no denying the fact that there have been too few tangible rewards to the students who excel as readers. Seldom does one see in a public

---

[11] Hyman G. Rickover, *Education and Freedom* (New York: E. P. Dutton & Co., Inc., 1956).

[12] American Association for the Advancement of Science, *Report on Broad Improvements in Science Teaching,* "Science Education News," 1962.

distinguish between academic-professional work and clerical tasks. Examples of the former would be selecting library materials, working with teachers in assembling materials for teaching units, cataloging materials that have not been precataloged, doing reading, counseling, and reference work with students and faculty, developing displays of library materials, working with student library clubs, working with librarians in other libraries in the community on interlibrary-use problems, presenting book review programs, and studying and doing research on library problems. Much of this work is done behind the scenes and is not observable by the public.

6. The belief that librarians and teachers couldn't be trusted to choose books for the library without being made conscious of the need for exercising proper caution lest the school and community become embroiled in controversy over the presence of some books that might offend certain individuals and groups. Librarians in the United States have faced severe and constant difficulties since the mid-1940's over the question of censorship and the right of access to books. The files of the American Library Association Committee on Intellectual Freedom contain many instances in which school and public librarians fought off the attacks of aggressive but misguided censors—with a conspicuous lack of help from school administrators either at the state or the national level. These instances are well-known in the library profession; they explain why librarians are likely to be bitter when administrators try to control book-selection policies in the schools. This is not to say that librarians are always wise or judicious in their defense of specific titles. Their situation is not unlike that of the American Association of University Professors which, in the defense of academic freedom, sometimes finds itself defending individuals who, in certain respects, are not altogether admirable.

7. The belief that the concept of a library should be restricted to printed books and should not include all types of carriers, or media, of information. Both librarians and school administrators debated this question with an unusual lack of understanding until the 1960's, when it became clear to both parties that the concept of a library has always changed when a new kind of medium was invented. Librarians were too stubborn in their defense of the printed word, and administrators were too quick to assume that books were "old-fashioned," and that audiovisual materials possessed some magical

school corridor an exhibit case containing a golden medal awarded to Peter Egghead for being the outstanding reader of good books in the class of 1965. Seldom does one see an exhibit mentioning winners of the National Merit Awards and other achievement scholarships!

## The Home and the Community

The home and the community have not stressed the value of reading in such a way as to impress young people with a sense of its importance. Rather, the teen-ager has witnessed his community leaders finding money for gymnasiums, well-equipped home economics, sewing, and food-preparation rooms, well-equipped shops for vocational education, expensive band instruments and uniforms, and fully outfitted athletic teams at the same time they said there was no money for books. Youth has usually been able to see that where the community's dollars go, there go its deepest interests.

## Outmoded Concepts

Although concepts frequently outgrow the realities upon which they are based, they may continue to have as much influence as if the reality still existed. Anyone who has been a part of the university community during the middle of the twentieth century must be aware that progress in bringing about reforms in most aspects of the field of education is seriously hampered by the outmoded concepts that are commonly stated. This has been particularly true of the school library field. As long as some of these concepts dominate the thinking of individuals and groups, progress in improving school library service could not be made. The most serious of these were:

1. Most school administrators, by virtue of their training and the nature of the men attracted to the work, could not be fully sympathetic to the needs of a school library because it was an essential element in the world of traditional learning—a world foreign to many administrators. (This concept originated in the conditions described earlier.) Conscientious efforts on the part of administrators themselves, plus the development of conditions in American society which enabled faculties of departments and colleges of education to prepare their graduates in both academic and professional subjects, plus the fact that the American public has raised its standards of

what it expects of the school administrators, have all helped to correct this situation. The enrichment of the old teachers colleges by transforming them into broader-based institutions (more nearly like liberal arts colleges and universities) also helped. Efforts to place the study of all professional subjects, including education, at the graduate level helped to guarantee in graduates a strong academic background as well as a thorough professional training.

Failure to appreciate the conditions under which school administrators must work, as stated by Burbank,[13] has created an unfair image of the reading habits of administrators. Cultural reading—as contrasted with reading for the acquisition of information—is one of the quieter arts that seem to thrive best when the individual is unharried, untroubled, and more or less at peace with himself and with his environment. This condition is seldom achieved by school administrators.

2. School administrators refused to delegate to librarians the authority to run the libraries as they and the teachers wanted them run. This probably developed out of the unwillingness of the administrators to establish a specific fund for the purchase of the books and other library materials and to put it under the control of the librarian. There were many reasons for the administrators' reluctance in this matter, including the real fear of community reaction to the presence of questionable books in the school libraries (*Catcher in the Rye* and *Dictionary of American Slang* were two titles that caused much trouble in the 1960's), the real or fancied incapabilities of school librarians, the issuance of "recommended" lists by state departments of education, and purchasing requirements that did not permit wise book-buying methods. An example of such requirements would be the forcing of selection at one time of year only—from exhibits at annual meetings of the state education association. In the larger city school systems, the selection of library materials was usually delegated to the school library supervisors; but, in the small systems, the administrators' fears were frequently justified.

3. The belief that the combined study hall-library would increase student reading. The assumption was that if the student were forced to go to the school library to study his own books, he might be in-

---

[13] Burbank, *op. cit.*

fluenced by the library books. This is sound theory but it failed to take into account the resistance students generated against being forced to do their studying in this manner. One need only visit such a library to see how it prevents the kind of use of the library that was intended.

4. The belief that central elementary or secondary school libraries were unnecessary if generous provisions for classroom collections were made. This concept has pretty well lost its force for secondary school libraries, but it is still vigorously promoted by administrators in the elementary school field. In fact, one of the first projects undertaken by the Knapp School Library Project was the establishment of two elementary school library demonstrators, one in the Central Park Elementary School in Plainview, N.Y., and one in the Marcus Whitman Elementary School in Richland, Washington. The problem in this outmoded concept was that elementary school administrators seemed unable to understand how a central elementary school library could do anything that could not be done with a classroom collection. Or, to put it another way, what could a school librarian possibly know that a classroom teacher wouldn't? The Knapp demonstration answered this question in a way that abstract arguments could not. The special knowledge a school librarian possesses is her knowledge of reference books, indexes, and catalogs, her ability to translate the reader's needs into the terminology used in indexes and bibliographies, her knowledge of the contents of books, and her ability to guide readers in their choice of reading materials. School librarians have assumed that the existence of central school libraries does not eliminate the need for classroom collections, especially at the elementary level.

5. The belief that the principal duties of school librarians consisted of what librarians thought of as clerical housekeeping—typing catalog cards, stamping "date due" slips for books being charged in and out, paging books and periodicals from the shelves when students want them, keeping order in the study hall, and so on. Unfortunately, too many examples can be found to justify this outmoded concept. Where professional librarians are found doing this kind of work, one of two things is usually true: either the librarian is the wrong kind of person, or she is forced to do this type of work because of lack of clerical help or because the physical layout of the library is wrong. School librarians are taught in library schools to

quality which made them automatically "better" as teaching materials. All these points of view are expressed in the following statement issued by the University of Colorado in 1962:

### Film: The New Language

Film, young though it is in comparison with the other arts, is the most compelling and absorbing attraction of our time. It is as exciting to this generation as the theater, the printed page, and the songs of the minstrels were to the people of preceding centuries.

Film, like the printed word, is a powerful means of communication, but where the latter allows the reader to participate in an imagined world of other people, places, and circumstances, film seems to bring the viewer immediately into a living world being projected before him. Its moving images, edited into a meaningful sequence, together with the spoken words, sound effects, and music, are a new language vastly different from that of the printed word.

Since it is a new language, those who want to understand and appreciate it must learn its elements. Instead of passively seeing films, it is necessary for us to observe the ways in which the film maker arranges scenes, conveys time and space, uses the camera, lighting, sound, and so on, if we are fully to comprehend his intentions, be it a feature, experimental, animated, informational, sponsored, or documentary film that he has created.

In order to gain a deeper appreciation of this . . . unique medium, we should also know something of its history, become acquainted with some of its outstanding directors, photographers, and so on, and be aware of the range of its possibilities. So the films on this program have been selected in the hope that they will stimulate a more intense interest in film as an exciting art form and medium of communication. They will include both old and new examples of the filmmaker's art, films on techniques, and films about the development of the motion picture camera.[14]

In the second paragraph, the writer of this statement shows the basic lack of understanding of what a piece of writing is, or of how it communicates, that is found so often among audiovisual experts and school administrators. The fallacy lies in the lack of realization that the *imagined world of other people* which the writer presents has, if the work is a great piece of writing, the same reality the film producer creates when he *brings the viewer immediately into a living world being projected before him*. To be sure, the language is different, and neither can be appreciated without long and careful

---

[14] Department of Audiovisual Education, "Film, the New Language," (Boulder: University of Colorado, 1962).

study. But this does not mean that one form is necessarily better than the other. Both convey knowledge and thus should be used interchangeably in the library in much the same spirit that a student of music may study the score of a symphonic composition while he listens to a stereophonic recording through earphones. No one would say that one is "better" than the other.

Fortunately, this question was resolved in the early 1960's and school libraries began to be thought of as the place where all the carriers of information were collected, stored, and used.[15] To express this new concept, it was sometimes necessary to use various forms of jargon such as *materials center, resources center, instructional media center,* and so on, but soon these long and clumsy terms were replaced again by the simple, short, well-understood, and dignified word *library.* The question, however, of the proper ratio between dollars spent for audiovisual materials and dollars spent for books to achieve equal educational returns remained unanswered for a long time.

As representative of a somewhat conservative, but nonetheless prevalent point of view toward the use of films, the following essay by a newspaper columnist does make a point that was frequently forgotten—namely, the power of words to express a complex concept quickly:

### Nothing Has Been Invented to Take the Place of Reading

We have exaggerated and blown up out of all proportion our audiovisual system of education. If this seems too reactionary or conservative a statement, let me say that if we are able to institute the audiovisual system of education in every American school, we would make of all our teachers high-class mechanics and thus, the profession of a teacher, the noblest profession in the world, would come to a speedy end.

The audiovisual system is simply an extension of our hurry-up attitudes. It takes a long time to read a book and we are afraid if we don't understand the book at once our time will be wasted. We have entirely too much concern about making books assimilable. Every man is better for reading a book he doesn't understand.

When I was a boy on the lower East Side of New York City, we used to meet each other and ask: "Have you read it yet?" We were talking of Victor Hugo's *Les Miserables.* We knew it was an important book and that it would have a profound influence on us so

---

[15] Francis Henne, "Structuring Library Education Curriculums for Preparing Librarians of Material Centers," in *The School Library as a Materials Center.* U.S. Office of Education Circular No. 708 (Washington, D.C.: USGPO, 1963), 53–60.

we went in training to read it. It was a happy day when we were able to answer, "Well, I read it."

There is a great difference between reading *Les Miserables* and seeing Frederic March and Charles Laughton in a rerun movie on the late show. You could watch March and Laughton twenty times over and you still wouldn't know a thing about the book. There are no short-cuts: you must read it. There is a relationship between the eye and the printed word that defies coherent explanation.

Carl Sandburg, in his biography of Abraham Lincoln, mentions that men in both the Confederate and Union armies read *Les Miserables*. They read it in a cheap, pirated edition called "the Volunteer's edition." So widespread was the book's popularity that these soldiers would call each other the names they borrowed from Hugo's characters. Over the tough winter of 1864, the Confederate soldiers nicknamed themselves "Lee's Miserables."

No matter how artfully the audiovisual interpretation presents *Les Miserables,* it will not pay off. You will not remember that Hugo wrote: "Every man a property-owner and not one a master." Nor will you remember that in one of his introductions he wrote: "I banish poverty, I instruct ignorance, I heal sickness, I hate hatred, this is where I stand and this is why I wrote *Les Miserables.*"

You are alone when you read this and you cannot duplicate the same process in a mass audience. When you are in a mass audience, you gain anonymity; when you read you gain an enlarged identity. You learn different things and in a different way. Trying to learn everything the same way is like learning the multiplication table and trying to determine the physical laws of earth with it.

The great fact about a book is that it preserves errors as well as truth. This is what audiovisual education will never do. It will never be as independent of the censors as the book is.[16]

In his enthusiasm for the book, Mr. Golden probably overstates his case, just as does the writer for the defense of films presented earlier.

8. The belief that an instructional program in which the organized teaching aspects are carefully planned and executed will necessarily result in the best kind of learning environment for high school students.

The library has traditionally been thought of as the place where the individual reader is on his own, free of all elements that regiment his time, his pace, and his reading paths. Thus, it was natural that academic librarians would respond with enthusiasm to the revolt against the excessive paternalism of school and college teaching

---

[16] Harry Golden, "Nothing Has Been Invented to Take the Place of Reading," in *The Carolina Israelite*, May 14, 1961.

in the 1950's and 1960's, a revolt which expressed itself under the banners of honors programs and independent study. Furthermore, because it was obvious that the new learning materials—educational television, teaching machines, phonograph- and tape-recordings, and language laboratories—could be used by individuals as well as by large groups, the student should expect to be able to use these machines alongside books, magazines, newspapers, pamphlets, government documents, and maps, all of which were the traditional materials found in libraries.

Some schools began to take cognizance of the fact that a shift in emphasis from teaching to learning (unless this remained a matter of toying with slogans) could increase the richness of the school instructional programs for those students who had the will to learn. (Colleges had worked along these lines for decades in their honors programs.) For example, the principal of the Jefferson High School, Jefferson County, Colorado, announced to the public on September 27, 1962, that the work of the school would be reorganized so that students would be divided into three groups, the first of which would be in organized classroom activities from nine to twelve, whereas during the afternoons students would spend their time in the library, the studios, and the laboratories. Other groups were organized along conventional lines. This was tangible recognition of the fact that schools could now begin to recognize various ways of learning, not just the classroom.

### Summary

Changes in ways of thinking about all the factors that had made the secondary school library as weak as it generally was at the middle of the twentieth century came to a head during this period. They resulted in a willingness to restudy the role of the secondary school library, and to make of it a teaching and learning instrument that would permit the schools to upgrade the quality of their instructional programs along the lines demanded by the American public. Two basic documents heralded the change: The American Association of School Libraries's *Standards for School Library Programs*[17] (1960) and the Educational Facilities Laboratory's *The School Library* (1963).[18]

---

[17] American Association of School Libraries, *Standards for School Library Programs* (Chicago: American Library Association, 1960).

[18] Ellsworth and Wagener, *op. cit.*

# CHAPTER III

# The Terminology of Communication

## The Language of Communication

Although creatures lower in the scale of evolution than the primates have methods of communication,[1] only man seems to have developed a complicated language and a method of recording his knowledge so that he can store and accumulate a body of information and principles that enable him to gain a measure of control over his environment.

The methods man has used for recording his knowledge have changed many times: from primitive carvings on the walls of caves; to carvings on stone, wooden, and clay tablets; to writing on tablets, leaves, scrolls, and sheets of paper bound together in volumes; to photo-images on films, slides, filmstrips; to electronic impulses transmitted by wire or by air and recorded on tapes and cylinders of various kinds.

Each of these methods has had its advantages and disadvantages. Some, like the clay tablets and the scrolls, have been discarded as being too heavy and clumsy to use. Some, like the motion picture film, are costly to make and can be used only with intermediary machines and are best adaptable for use by groups rather than by individuals. Some, like the printed book, are highly adaptable and mobile as well as inexpensive to make, but cannot be used unless one has learned to read the particular language of the writer.

Some, like the printed book, can be produced by a single man. Some, like the motion picture film, require a large organization, with much capital and machinery, before they can be produced.

Some, like the motion picture film, employ a vocabulary that transcends the limits of nationality or language; others, like the printed book, are limited in use to those who have mastered the particular language of the writer and who have undergone the disci-

---

[1] Karl von Fresch, "Dialects in the Language of the Bees," *Scientific American* (August 1962), 78–79.

pline of learning how to extract meaning from the written word.

Motion picture films, which introduce few barriers between the reality they portray and the viewer, have their own style, which may be simple and easily understood by everyone (e.g., a Micky Mouse film), or may be highly sophisticated and understandable only to those who have learned the style of the director (e.g., an Ingemar Bergman movie, or the so-called creative films of the 1960's).

Books, too, have their own style, which range in comprehensibility from a collection of simple nursery rhymes to such complex works as Joyce's *Ulysses,* for which the reader—if he is to get out of it all the writer put in—must have a wide background of experience and knowledge. To read a simple book requires very little background, but to read a complex book one must be well educated. For example, one can read the words in Dante's *Divine Comedy* and understand most of them, and he can absorb the story or the plot; yet, unless he knows something of the Middle Ages, its history and people, the *Divine Comedy* is almost completely meaningless. By the same token, a simply written lyric poem can be read at several levels of comprehension, but its full power is felt only by those who have mastered all the elements of literary style as well as the background of human experience.

The range in styles of the written word (from *Peter Rabbit* to Kant's *Critique of Pure Reason*) is wider than the ranges offered by other media of communication—art and music—because language is the most flexible and complex of the media. It is complex in the sense that it can express a given thought in a single word or in an elaborate sequence of ideas (e.g., a philosophic argument). Words not only have specific meanings, but they also have connotations of a highly sophisticated nature. Thus, the imagery of the poetry of the 1950's made the poetry meaningless to those who did not learn the vocabulary of the imagery. On the other hand, one could, in the same period, listen to an Ives symphony and enjoy the rhythm, melody, and harmony without understanding the pattern or style or specific method of the composition.

This point is presented as a factor in understanding the role of the school library because there has been a tendency in the schools to look to the audiovisuals as a quick and easy way to escape the drudgery of teaching students to read with comprehension. Learning to read is hard, whereas learning to look at a film *may* be easy.

Books containing the great classical traditions of the Western world would not be needed in the school libraries if the courses in literature failed to teach students the vocabularies of these writings. This may or may not be significant, depending on what one thinks civilization is.

## Storage of the Carriers of Communication

Once man accumulates the records of his knowledge, he faces the problem of storing and organizing them (regardless of the form) so that he can remember what he has learned and where it can be found. Of all the carriers of knowledge that man has invented, the book (sheets bound together in a volume) has proved to be the easiest to handle and to store, and—since the invention of printing from movable type—the least expensive to produce.

Western man has, since the days of ancient Rome, used the word *library* to designate the place where the records of his accumulated knowledge is kept.

Since it is man's accumulated and organized knowledge that has given him the power to accomplish all he has since he began to record his knowledge, it is quite natural that he transfers some of his respect for the power of knowledge to the carrier of that knowledge (i.e., to books), and to the place where the carriers of knowledge are kept (i.e., to libraries). Books, by their very nature, can be beautiful as objects, and type design has been one of the arts for over five hundred years. A roll of film, a video tape, or a phonograph record can never, in itself, become an object of beauty and reverence, even though it may contain knowledge of greater power, beauty, and usefulness than any printed book.

The reverence and respect man pays to books and libraries as symbols of the power of knowledge can be found in every college and university worthy of the name. The library is usually the most impressive and the most monumental, in the architectural sense, of the academic buildings. It is usually given the central position among the buildings, as a token of respect, as well as to facilitate its use.

The fact that in the secondary schools, in the first half of the twentieth century, the library was so noticeable for its absence or its insignificance was used by the school's critics as evidence of the school's lack of concern for traditional intellectual values. Whether this lack of concern was the fault of the educators or of the American public was debatable.

## The Proper Name for a Library

Whether a library should be called *library, scriptorium, bookery, resources center, teaching materials center, instructional materials center, learning center, libratory,* or some other jargon word-of-the-moment is, from one point of view, less important than the question of what the library actually does. By the same token, it may make little difference whether librarians are called *librarians, reading counselors,* or *information retrievers,* as long as they do what they are supposed to do. But if it is necessary to give up the venerable and universally known name *library* merely because the library now includes all forms of carriers of information, or because the library is now about to perform the function it should have been performing all along, then the victory—if it is that—would seem to be a Pyrrhic one.[2]

## The Proper Contents of a Library

There are many kinds of libraries, some (like the Lamont Library at Harvard) designed for undergraduate use; some (like the Huntington Library in California), for research; some (like the new Beineke Rare Book Library at Yale), for the housing of rare books; some (like the Midwest Interlibrary Center in Chicago), for the storage of little-used materials; some (like the Washington University Library in St. Louis), to serve all these functions. In the secondary school, the library exists to provide the sources for group teaching and for individual learning. It differs from a classroom collection in that it is larger, includes indexes, catalogs, and bibliographies, and is staffed by librarians who have been trained in handling information literature. It differs from the classroom, the laboratory, the shop, or the studio in the way the individual uses it. In the library, the individual is on his own; he gets no help from the staff unless he needs it and asks for it. He proceeds at his own pace, in his own way. He learns by himself, not as a member of a group.

2 Francis Henne, "Structuring Library Education Curriculums for Preparing Librarians of Material Centers," in *The School Library as a Materials Center.* U.S. Office of Education Circular No. 708 (Washington, D.C.: USGPO, 1963), 53–60.

The traditional materials found in libraries were books, magazines, newspapers, pamphlets, documents, manuscripts, maps, pictures, and slides. Microforms—microfilms, microcards, microfiche (translucent sheets of film with images of pages photographed on them), microprints—became common after 1931. Because motion picture films were designed for group use in the classroom, rather than for individual viewing, they were usually not put in libraries. But because of the wealth of information accumulated in documentary films, radio transcripts, and television tapes, it became clear by 1960 that the individual needed access to all the information he should have, regardless of the medium through which it was presented.[3]

For example, the bare facts of one of the most significant events of mid-century America—the assassination of President John F. Kennedy in November 1963—could be found by reading an account in *Time Magazine*. But to understand how and why this event affected the whole structure of American society so profoundly, one would need to look at the television presentation. No written account could convey the emotional power that came from watching the face of Mrs. Kennedy while Senator Mansfield read his eulogy to her late husband. Nor could one understand how this event broke down so much anti-Catholic prejudice unless he had participated in the funeral conducted by Cardinal Cushing. Here, as stated earlier in the quotation on film, the camera enabled one to experience the reality firsthand. Later, of course, the other art forms—tributes in essay form in *The Saturday Review, The Reporter,* and other books and magazines—captured the mood and significance of the event in a manner that was equally important.

Since about 1950, it has been understood, though not too frequently put into practice, that all carriers of information belong in the library, so that learners will not have to go to different places to use the different media. Colleges and universities realized this first. Purdue University placed responsibility for all audiovisual material on the Director of Libraries. Other colleges provided housing and use facilities for these materials in the library, sometimes bringing together—as a separate library department—a staff of media spe-

---

[3] C. W. Stone, "The Crisis in Education—A Mandate for Libraries," *American Library Association Bulletin* (February 1961), 122–28.

cialists. Library schools developed training programs so that librarians would understand how the new media were used.[4]

The kinds of information carriers available prior to 1960 were simple and primitive in comparison to those that have been developed since. The concept of programmed learning led to the development of teaching machines, which enable each person to move ahead at his own pace, and to learning exhibits—long used in museums—in which the written text, an oral description, and a physical demonstration are all combined into one effort to teach. The Sonora Desert Museum, near Tucson, Arizona, made excellent use of this technique to demonstrate the process of erosion and the benefits of conservation of the soil. Yet these and other forms of learning aids are all teaching devices. What happens in the minds of learners depends not so much on the input as on the efforts the learner makes to understand, to absorb, and to make over into his own understanding. This is a matter of learning, not teaching.

Since the professional training of a librarian equips her to be a specialist in knowing how to locate information in the carriers of information, her talent should not be limited to the information in printed books, but should be extended to all other forms as well. The audiovisual specialist who, in the early days of audiovisual materials, spent much of his time helping teachers learn how to use film and other audiovisual aids, now delegates this part of his work to the school librarian and concentrates his time and special knowledge on the creation of audiovisual materials. The evolution is a natural one.

It is well to remember that printed books are both "visual" and "audio." The reader absorbs their contents through his eyes and his ears. Books that have been read aloud onto tapes and phonograph records become audio aids. When the pages of a book are put on microfilm, they become a filmstrip and are a visual aid. When accompanied by a soundtrack, they become audiovisual aids. All motion picture films are based on a script which, if printed and bound, becomes a book.

In short, as Miss Stein might have said, a library is a library is a library is a library!

---

[4] Henne, *op. cit.*

# CHAPTER IV

# The Concept of a School Library

## Definitions[1]

The term *school library* has several definitions, each one reflecting different points of view:

1. A school library is a system for making sources of information available.

2. A school library is a place containing carriers of information, a staff, and furniture and equipment, to which the learner may go for the information he needs to educate himself according to the instructional program of his school and his own needs.

3. A school library is a sanctuary where the individual who is willing to make the effort, and who knows how, may communicate directly with the recorded thoughts of men and women through the ages.

4. A school library is a laboratory in which the learner may work out the experiments in thinking necessary to test the concepts to which his teachers have introduced him, much as he works out physics theories in the physics laboratory. The library-laboratory instruments are the bibliographies and catalogs; the materials are the recorded memories of man stored in the form of books and other materials; the methods are the intellectual disciplines of scholarship; the "laboratory assistant" is the librarian. The teaching program of the school can be judged effective, not only when the students have demonstrated—through the passing of examinations —that they have acquired a given amount of education, but also when the students can prove that they can, without the help of teachers, counselors, advisers, testers, or librarians, go to the storehouse of man's knowledge and get out of it the information they

---

[1] Francis Henne, "Toward Excellence in School Library Programs," in *New Definitions of School Library Service* (Chicago: The University of Chicago Press, 1960).

need to solve a problem, or to write a report, and then demonstrate their ability to think as an adult is required to think.

5. A school library is the intellectual center of the school, to which everyone—administrators, teachers, and students—must come for the materials of learning.

6. A school library is a place where one may go between classes to study one's own textbooks.

7. A school library is a kind of intellectual chapel, the one place in the school where one works alone, without help from others.

As can be seen from these definitions, there are many ways of thinking about the purpose of a school library. But common to all are certain basic ideas:

—the bond between the individual and his heritage;

—the individual—rather than group—quality of activity;

—the independent learning—self-teaching;

—the respect or reverence for the record of man's ideas.

## School Libraries: Their Character and Service

Who determines the nature and character of school libraries? And what are the conditions that must exist if good library service is to be given?

In theory the public, expressing its wishes through local boards of education, tells the school administration what the nature of the school library shall be. In fact, this has usually *not* been the case. More important have been the specific ideas of the school administrators or school librarians. Sometimes faculty committees, architects, community organizations, officials of the state departments of education, members of the local university's department of education, or sometimes state accrediting agencies have been the dominating factor. But regardless of where the concept originates, the school administration bears the sole responsibility for following it through —for providing the staff and the physical facilities, and for maintaining the proper interrelations and working conditions among the school personnel that nurture and sustain a good school library.

## The Right Kind of Librarian

Without the right kind of librarian, a school library seldom becomes more than a glorified study hall. This is true not just of school libraries but of public, college, university, and special libraries as well. Without someone to select, organize, interpret, and promote the use of library materials, they remain a static resource.

*Basic educational background.* A school librarian should have a liberal arts college education with a major in one of the academic subjects—preferably history or literature—with basic courses in science, the social sciences, and the other humanities. She should have done independent reading in the history of ideas because one of the questions students frequently ask her is the place of an author or a book title in the development of Western civilization. A master's degree in her major field is highly desirable. The school librarian should be one of the best-educated members of the teaching staff.

*Professional training.* A school librarian should have a basic knowledge of librarianship and education. The subjects she must study are bibliography and reference, book selection and organization, and the use of audiovisual techniques and materials. The basic mastery of this material occupies at least one year of graduate study. A library school graduate who is intelligent and well educated, and who possesses good personality and character traits, should bring to the teaching program a specialized knowledge of the literature of scholarship that supplements and complements the specialized knowledge of the various subjects possessed by the faculty. No one librarian can be a master of the literature of all fields. She should, however, know the reference and bibliographic tools in all fields, plus a good deal about the important books in at least one field.

She will also be expected to have had basic training in education and will be required in most states to have a teaching certificate. She will be expected to know something of the history and philosophy of public education, the psychology of youth, the methods of teaching, plus as much else as she has time to learn about public school administration.

In the larger schools, there will be a place on the school library staff for librarians with specialized training in various fields—audiovisual materials or reading counseling, for instance—or specialized knowledge of the literature of a particular subject or group of subjects, but the small and medium-sized schools seldom can afford such specialists.[2]

*Personality traits.*   The traits that make a good school librarian are basically the same ones that make a good teacher or a good principal. A good school librarian is:

1. A person who takes real satisfaction in helping individual students develop a love for learning and for reading;
2. A person with an intelligent mind that insists on growing through the reading of books;
3. A person who manages to be so approachable that even the shyest of students will not hesitate to go to her for help;
4. A person whose knowledge of the contents of books shows as a radiating enthusiasm for books;
5. A person who is aggressive enough to go more than halfway in establishing relationships with classroom teachers so that they will be convinced she can help them to assemble appropriate library materials for teaching; a person who possesses the knack of knowing when a student needs help but is afraid to ask her for it;
6. A person who is well enough organized to learn how to run a library easily.

## What a Librarian Does

*Selection of materials.*   The librarian selects books and other learning materials for the library, some of which are purchased from the book fund established by the administration but controlled by the librarian and an advisory committee of teachers and audiovisual experts, and some of which come as gifts. In selecting books, she works constantly with the teachers—and, indeed, encourages them to take the initiative in the selection process. The librarian bears the responsibility of seeing that the proper selection is made, regardless of the method used.[3]

---

[2]Alice Lohrer, "School libraries as Instructional Materials Centers, with Implications for Training: A Progress Report of This Study Under Title VIII, National Defense Education Act"; E. T. Schofield, "Competencies Needed by School Librarians for Selecting and Organizing Materials Center"; and K. I. Taylor, "Competencies Needed by School Librarians for Planning Quarters and Administrating the Use of Materials Center, in *The School Libraries as a Materials Center.* U.S. Office of Education Circular No. 708 (Washington, D.C.: USGPO, 1963), 12–24.

[3] Martin Roseoff, *The Library in High School Teaching* (New York: H. W. Wilson Co., 1955); and A. M. Wofford, *The School Library at Work* (New York: H. W. Wilson Co., 1959).

In addition to selecting the books and audiovisual materials that are purchased for the teaching program of the library, the librarian will draw upon her special knowledge of bibliography to acquire pamphlets, government documents, and other types of material that make up a rich library collection.

From her discussions with students on their reading problems, the librarian will learn about gaps in the collection that should be filled.

In building the collection, the librarian should be fully aware of the problems involved with censorship and with freedom of access to materials as stated in the American Library Association *Bill of Rights:*

> The Council of the American Library Association reaffirms its belief in the following basic policies which should govern the services of all libraries:
>
> 1. As a responsibility of library service, books and other reading matter selected should be chosen for values of interest, information, and enlightenment of all the people of the community. In no case should any book be excluded because of the race or nationality, or the political or religious views of the writer.
>
> 2. There should be the fullest practicable provision of material presenting all points of view concerning the problems and issues of our time, international, national, and local; and books or other reading matter of sound factual authority should not be proscribed or removed from library shelves because of partisan or doctrinal disapproval.
>
> 3. Censorship of books, urged or practiced by volunteer arbiters of morals or political opinion or by organizations that would establish a coercive concept of Americanism, must be challenged by libraries in maintenance of their responsibility to provide public information and enlightenment through the printed word.
>
> 4. Libraries should enlist the cooperation of allied groups in the fields of science, of education, and of book publishing in resisting all abridgement of the free access to ideas and full freedom of expression that are the tradition and heritage of Americans.
>
> 5. As an institution of education for democratic living, the library should welcome the use of its meeting rooms for socially useful and cultural activities and discussion of current public questions. Such meeting places should be available on equal terms to all groups in the community regardless of the beliefs and affiliations of their members.[4]

---

[4] "The Library Bill of Rights," *American Library Association Bulletin,* (November 1953), 485.

In carrying out these suggested responsibilities, the librarian should be conscious of the degrees of maturity of the students, of the difference between school libraries and other kinds of libraries, and of social policies. With good judgment and tact, the librarian's freedom to select materials is a school asset of great importance: without them, no bill of rights can ward off trouble in the community.

*Organization of materials.* The librarian processes and organizes the library materials for use. Before about 1960, these duties appeared to occupy much, if not most, of the time of the library staff. But since that time, centralized processing methods and available published lists have altered the picture. Most of the books a school library buys have already been cataloged by the Library of Congress or by the H. W. Wilson Company, and catalog cards can be purchased with the books through commercial agencies. The books can even be purchased with call numbers stamped on their spines and with charging cards and book pockets all ready for use. Although the librarians will sometimes wish to prepare more subject-heading cards than are furnished by these systems, the amount of time that must be devoted to the cataloging operation by the professional librarian is relatively small. No longer is it necessary, or even desirable, for high-quality librarians to spend their valuable time doing cataloging work, for it is already done. Large-city school library systems have provided this service to their schools for decades, and several state and regional processing operations were organized in the 1960's.

School libraries will sometimes acquire books (usually local imprints) for which they must do the original cataloging, and some of the nonbook material will require special attention. Pamphlets, so-called ephemeral materials, and audiovisual materials cannot always be handled as efficiently as printed books can, but printed lists and guides for these materials are available.

It has been the custom for secondary schools (probably because of lack of funds) to keep files of unbound periodicals—usually in closed stacks not available directly to students. Sometimes each periodical issue was protected by a special pamphlet cover, thus preserving the life of the issue. Library staff members brought these separate issues to readers upon demand. This practice was in direct contrast to that followed by college and public libraries, which bound annual volumes of the periodicals and placed them out on open shelves where readers could have direct access to them. The secondary school library practice was not only more expensive and wasteful of staff time, but it was also a source of frustration to readers. Introduction of the Xerox-914 photocopiers in 1961–63 enabled schools to supply inexpensive photocopies of periodical articles and of pages from books for those who needed to do their work away from the library itself.

*Supervisory duties.* The librarian supervises a staff of assistants (professionals, clerical assistants, and student workers). She and the other professionals do the same kind of work. The clerical staff does the housekeeping—charging out books, shelving books, stamping library ownership marks on books, typing catalog cards and filing them, preparing pamphlets for use, and other tasks that can be learned quickly.

*Reference work.* The librarian and her professional assistants spend as much time as possible doing what is called *reference work* —that is, helping students learn how to translate an unformulated need for information into terminology which can be used to get at the information in the reference books. This involves teaching the use of the reference books, which are a specialized kind of book. Although she may, when the occasion demands, find the information the student needs, her first responsibility is to teach the student how to find it himself. In doing this, the librarian has an opportunity to introduce the student to a book called *List of Subject Headings,* which contains the highly organized network of the terminology of scholarship as found in the Library of Congress.

Most of the teaching has to be done on an individual basis, as the problems arise, but some can be done in a group-instruction situation. It should be done by the librarian, not the classroom teacher, because—with rare exceptions—the teacher does not have enough specialized knowledge about bibliographies, reference books, and subject headings to do an adequate and accurate job of teaching their use.

*Relation to faculty.* The librarian works with the faculty—individual members and departments—in selecting books. Together, they study book lists, bibliographies, publishers' catalogs, book reviews, as well as other special sources, and agree on the books that should be purchased or borrowed from other libraries for teaching purposes.[5]

They also work together in assembling material for special projects in the library itself, or in classrooms, laboratories, studios, or instructional centers. Using book trucks, the librarian and a teacher may assemble a group of books and films and other materials that are then sent to the classroom for the duration of a project or unit of instruction. In the larger schools, the library may maintain subbranches in various parts of the building. These may be small and unorganized, or large and formal. They are sometimes called *instructional centers.*[6]

Sometimes the librarian will help the teachers with their own personal projects. This will ordinarily be true if the school's professional library for teachers is a part of the school library. The librarian will be on the lookout for reports of new research projects that may be of interest to the teachers but that are published in sources outside their regular orbit of inspection.

*Preparation of special materials.* The librarian prepares reading lists, special bibliographies, and news bulletins, and she develops displays designed to attract the students' attention and lead them to materials they would otherwise not know about.

*Other duties.* The librarian also confers with the school principal or superintendent on special needs and problems, prepares annual budget estimates, and supplies the administration with information needed to convince the school board—and, through its members, the entire community—of the need for adequate support for the school library.

She works with the staff of counselors, either soliciting information they have that she needs in working with students, or for giving them information *she* may have that would help them to understand a particular student.

She works with an advisory faculty library committee on the

---

[5] J. W. Brown, R. B. Lewis, and F. F. Hardervood, *Instruction: Materials and Methods* (New York: McGraw-Hill, Inc., 1959); J. J. Farley, "The High School Library as a Curriculum Center," *Clearing House,* Vol. 34, No. 3 (November 1959); Patricia Knapp, "The Monteith Experiments," *College and Research Libraries* (July 1961), 257–258; and National Citizens Council for Better Schools, *How Good are Our Teaching Materials?* (New York: The Council, 1958).

[6] J. Lloyd Trump, *Images of the Future: A New Approach to Secondary Education* (Urbana, Ill.: Commission on the Experimental Study of the Utilization of the Staff in the Secondary School, 1959).

formation of library policies, and with a student library club on special projects such as book collecting, printing presses, and the like. She also attends faculty and committee meetings, conferences, and works on school and community projects.

The librarian studies her professional journals and new books so that she may know about desirable practices other libraries have developed. She carries on research projects of her own so as to contribute to the state of knowledge in her own field, and she reads as much as she can during the day and assumes that she is expected to spend much of her after-school time reading. Librarianship is professional work. That means that the individual devotes her whole life to it, not just forty hours a week.

The librarian also works with other library agencies. Although all types of libraries in each community or state have usually worked together harmoniously, the demand for more library service by school students in the 1960's forced school, city, college, and state agency librarians into active programs of coordination. The American Library Association conference-within-a-conference in the summer of 1963 dramatized the need for such coordination. Steps began to be taken to draw the city public libraries and school libraries into more active cooperation. College and university libraries were on the fringes of this problem because their libraries were usually already overtaxed by their own swollen enrollments. Nevertheless, by means of photoduplication services, they were able to supply some of the research-type materials not ordinarily found in the school and public libraries.

Catalogs of motion picture films, television tapes, and filmstrips, distributed by university audiovisual departments, helped considerably in solving this problem.

### The Physical Setting[7]

The typical school library built before 1960 consisted of a rectangular room, with bookshelves on the walls and rows of tables and chairs in the middle of the room. Usually there was a formidable charging desk located front center, where it caused a maximum amount of distraction to the readers. There was also a small office for the librarian (usually with glass walls so that she could super-

[7] See the various publications of Educational Facilities Laboratories, Inc., listed in the bibliography.

vise the readers), a small conference room, and sometimes a seminar room.

During the 1920's, one occasionally found a library consisting of two rooms with a charging desk and library office marking the division. One room was a study hall, the other was the library. The librarian was expected to supervise the study hall as well as to perform the duties of a librarian.      •

Librarians have discovered that a library of this kind has no special character that might win the affection of its readers. It was not conceived as a gracious reading-living room. It contained rectangular study tables and straight-backed study chairs, and that was all.

Since the books were kept on shelves around the sides of the room, each person wanting a book had to walk past readers to get at the books. This source of distraction helped to create a mood of noise and confusion. Students assumed that the library was a place for visiting and talking, and in most libraries that was just what they did.

There was no privacy in these libraries, no place where the individual felt that the school trusted him enough to allow him to work in peace and seclusion without distraction. There was no place where he could leave his own books and notes when he left the room. Supervision was a kind of game between the librarian and the students to see who could outguess the other.

There was no architectural character or dignity or individuality in these libraries. They seemed to be designed as a kind of reading prison in which student misbehavior could be kept to a minimum by a librarian who could see everything that went on in the library as she sat in her office.

But, largely under the influence of Educational Facilities Laboratories, Inc. (established in the late 1950's to help institutions plan better physical facilities), a new conception of the physical setting for the school library began to take form in the 1960's. A second influence was the large number of fine and imaginative college library buildings that had been built since World War II—such as at Baldwin-Wallace College, Harvard University, Barnard College, Colgate University, Canisius College, Cornell University, Carleton College, and others (see Chapter II). The influence of the college libraries on secondary school libraries in the 1960's was significant. Some of the architects who had designed the better college libraries

—Murphy and Mackey, Perkins and Will, Moore and Hutchins, Hobart Wagener, Kilham, O'Connor, Caudill, to mention only a few—also worked on public school design. The college buildings were carefully studied by school administrators, who borrowed and adapted much of what they saw to the peculiar needs of the high schools.

The atmosphere of the new school libraries became that of a gracious home living room, with various kinds of reading facilities to meet the several needs and moods of different readers. Flat-top tables and straight chairs; individual reading-room carrels; group-study and conversation rooms for two to four readers; lounge-type chairs into which the reader could sink for undisturbed reading of a good book; conference and seminar rooms; viewing rooms for individual and small-group use of films; listening booths with earphones for record- and tape-listening; individual study booths for radio and television reception as well as for the use of teaching machines; diorama programmed learning displays; rooms for use of typewriters, calculating machines, slide and filmstrip projectors— all these facilities were found in the newer school libraries.[8]

The keynote and the central idea of the new libraries was privacy for the individual to study independently—without distraction, interruptions, or annoyance from group behavior—among the books he intended to use.

Architects were allowed to give the library real character through the imaginative use of design, color, materials, arrangement, and lighting. No longer was the library restricted to a box-shaped area (see the school libraries in Naperville, Illinois; Newton, Massachusetts; West Leyden, Illinois), or even to a one-floor-level plan. The new concept implied that the student could be trusted to work in the library with a feeling of pride, dignity, and purpose, and with due respect for the rights of other readers. Supervision was taken care of by the students themselves, who went to the library to work, not just to waste a little time between classes.

The noise level in these libraries was neither that of a bus depot nor that of a funeral home, but that of an active scientific laboratory where important problems are to be solved and new discoveries made.

---

[8] L. M. Stolurow, *Teaching by Machines*. U.S. Office of Education Cooperative Research Monograph No. 6 (Washington, D.C.: USGPO, 1961).

Because the new concept of a library assumed that its contents included all types of learning devices and all types of carriers of knowledge, the new libraries had to provide storage rooms for much electronic equipment as well as electrical outlets throughout the reading rooms, so that portable radio and television receivers, record-players and tape-recorders, and teaching machines could be charged out at the library circulation desk, taken to a study carrel, and used for varying lengths of time. Provision for access to closed-circuit and regular television cables was built into the new buildings.[9]

The librarians had to become skilled in the use of this machinery, but this skill proved to be relatively simple to learn and could be taught to student assistants on the job. The problem of maintenance, however, proved to be complex and to require highly skilled experts. Audiovisual experts were needed to create and to maintain specialized learning materials and to coordinate them with other elements in the teaching process. The qualifications of these experts were similar to those of the librarians. Because the material used in the machines became a part of the literature of knowledge, one learned about them in the same way be learned about books.

Stereophonic record-players with earphones provided such high-quality sound reception that planners no longer needed to build costly, soundproof listening rooms. Listening equipment could be located anywhere in the library. "Listening classrooms" and "previewing rooms," in which teachers taught from records and tapes, became necessary.

Student response to the new concept of a school library proved to be as satisfactory in the high schools as it had been in the dozens of colleges that had adopted the new concept years earlier. The new buildings proved what architects and wise teachers had always known: namely, that physical environment conditions behavior, and that youth will live up to a challenge if it is worthy and makes sense to them.

---

9 Educational Facilities Laboratories, Inc., *Study Carrells: Designs for Individual Study Space* (Stanford: The School Planning Laboratory, Stanford University, 1962).

## The Instructional Program Schedule
## of Student Time

One of the reasons the schools, prior to the 1960's, could manage to operate with libraries that seated less than 5 per cent of the enrolled students was that the libraries were not supposed to be used. The student's daily schedule, of five classroom periods a day, with one study hour and extracurricular activities, and the closing of the school library at four o'clock, came as close to guaranteeing nonuse of the library as it was possible to come without actually padlocking the library doors. Studying under the direct supervision of the classroom teacher was considered necessary and sufficient, as indeed it may have been.

But, as a result of several factors which came to the public's attention in the late 1950's, the schools began to see that they had grossly underestimated the capacity of students. As a result, they started following the college pattern of scheduling fewer class hours per day and assuming that students would study two to three hours for each hour of organized class instruction.

Three factors, in combination, made the idea of independent study attractive and possible: (1) the shortage of good teachers in the 1950's and 1960's, at a time when school enrollments were rising; (2) the introduction of the possibility of teaching by television, teaching machines, and programmed teaching devices;[10] and (3) the emphasis placed on academic excellence and on honors programs in the secondary schools as well as in the colleges.[11]

## An Adequate Budget Under
## the Control of the Librarian

As long as the school administrators kept tight and undelegated control over the library book fund, as well as over the selection of books, the school librarian could do no planning, nor could the faculty and the librarian together assemble an enlightened and use-

---

[10] Stolurow, *op. cit.;* H. H. Cassierer, *Television Teaching Today* (Paris, France: UNESCO, 1961); McGeorge Bundy, "Science as a Way of Life," *Harvard Today* (Autumn 1961), 23–24; B. F. Skinner, "Teaching Machines," *Scientific American* (November 1961), 91.

[11] See files of "The Superior Student," 1958. Published by the Interuniversity Committee on the Superior Student, Boulder, Colorado.

ful collection of instructional materials.[12] The fact that the American public has held school administrators personally responsible for almost everything that happened in the schools—including the use of books that offended the public—explained, in part, why administrators felt they had to keep close check on the library.

The adoption of objective standards by accrediting associations and by interested national associations, such as the American Library Association,[13] helped to convince school administrators of the wisdom of delegating to the librarian the authority to select books (something the larger city school systems had been doing for a quarter of a century).

A major shift in the concept of the size of a school library came about 1960. At that time, the American Association of School Libraries *Standards* was published, the Educational Facilities Laboratories, Inc., began to enter the field of school library planning, and world events forced schools to take a global approach to education.

Under the teaching conditions that prevailed in the first half of the twentieth century, there was no real reason why a school library with 1000–2000 books could not meet the demands that were placed on it. The student who paid close attention to what the teacher said in the class periods, and who read his textbook carefully, could fulfill his academic responsibilities successfully.

But the school that considered the classroom presentation merely as a point of departure, and that looked upon the textbook merely as an outline to be followed, needed larger libraries. City public libraries and college and university libraries began to be swamped with high school students after 1958. The problem became so critical that the president of the American Library Association selected as his theme for the 1963 Annual Conference the problems of the overlapping use of libraries by school students.

The problem of school size in relation to the number of books a school library required was a critical one. From the point of view of the individual student's intellectual growth, he needed access to a large library regardless of the number of students in his school. To a large extent, increased enrollments affected the number of duplicate books a library needed, not the number of titles it re-

---

12 Louis Shores, *Instructional Materials: An Introduction for Teachers* (New York: The Ronald Press Company, 1960).

13 American Association of School Librarians, *Standards for School Library Programs* (Chicago: American Library Association, 1960).

quired. But small school systems lacked the income necessary to support large libraries, just as they lacked the income to provide good laboratories, social science museums, or faculties with sufficient specialization to teach subjects properly. This was a major dilemma, the solution to which could not be found easily. Such a solution might include the consolidation of school districts into larger units and the use of state and federal aid.

A collection of 30,000 volumes in the school library was considered to be basic, if other community libraries were available to the high school students. School administrators were quick to see the need for that many books.

Suddenly the world that affected the life of each student contained all the peoples of the globe, not just those who lived in Western Europe, North America, the United States, or Cedar Rapids, Iowa. All at once, what happened in China became as important to the high school senior in Fargo, North Dakota, as what happened to the wheat crop in his state. The latest research in theoretical physics, that might have implications for space science and polar explorations, was likely to be given as much space in the daily newspapers as the wins and losses of the hometown baseball team.[14]

In short, new books and journals in large numbers became essential in the school library. The cost was high. A school library of 50,000 volumes that grew 5 per cent each year, when the average price of books was $6.00, would cost $300,000 for the basic collection and $15,000 for the annual additions. Annual library administrative costs might be more than twice as large as the fund for book purchases.

## A Philosophy of Education: Incentives and Rewards for Intellectual Excellence

Students, like other people, respect those values that the community of which they are a part values most highly. The student is surrounded by the symbols for success that the community believes in, and he responds to these symbols by trying to do those things that bring him the rewards which the symbols represent. For exam-

---

[14] Council of Chief State School Officers, *Purchase Guide for Programs in Science, Mathematics, and Modern Foreign Languages* (Boston: Ginn & Company, 1959).

ple, one of the first things one sees in a school building are the exhibit cases full of trophies won in athletic contests. Almost never does one see trophies representing high achievement for academic work (except possibly for debates and oratorical contests), for scholarships won by students, for outstanding term papers or reports.

Since the explosion of the first atomic bomb, respect for the work of the scientist has risen.[15] Advertisers used "the man in the white coat" to endorse their products. Seldom, however, have clergymen, journalists, high school teachers, librarians, or professors of history been used as endorsers. Not only did these people consider it improper to allow their names to be used, but presumably advertisers did not consider their potential appeal to be great. Otherwise they would have been used, just as the man in the white coat was used—anonymously, of course.

In the schools, the system of rewards reflects, as it should, the community's values. As has been noted, the men and women who, in the past, were promoted to school administrative posts, with high salaries, tended to be the successful coaches of athletic teams or the teachers of vocational subjects, not the teachers of English, history, or the social studies.

As long as the school's symbols for rewards were given for activities that were basically nonintellectual, activities that could be pursued without much study or mental effort, the school library did not thrive, nor did reading have much status among students. This, too, was a reflection of society's system of rewards. Success in the entertainment world, in business, in politics, and in athletics frequently was attained without the years of study and intellectual effort that involved the heavy use of recorded knowledge.

But the system of rewards began to change toward the end of the 1950's. Winners of National Merit Awards and other scholarships that recognized academic excellence were given much publicity in local newspapers.[16] Science fairs were covered thoroughly by the press, and pictures of prize-winning projects appeared in the papers. Musical performances of high quality reflected the excellent level of achievement in the arts, and so did the art exhibits. The amount

15 Bundy, *op. cit.*
16 James B. Conant, *Education and Liberty* (Cambridge, Mass.: Harvard University Press, 1953).

of space given in the local newspapers to events of this kind showed that the American public's interest in these achievements was high. The Kennedy Administration, with its emphasis on cultural achievement and its appeal to men and women of intellectual distinction, had a strong impact on the attitude of Americans toward intellectual achievement. (See editorials and columns following the assassination of the late President Kennedy in November 1963, in *The Atlantic, The Saturday Review, Harper's, The Reporter, Newsweek, The New Yorker* and other high-quality publications.)

School administrators, responding to the shift in public demand, introduced courses in Russian and stepped up the quality of teaching in the fields of languages, sciences, and mathematics. Several national associations of teachers of such subjects as biology, chemistry, physics, and mathematics appointed national commissions to improve the quality of teaching in those subjects and to prepare the new books that were needed.[17] Schools of education in various universities eliminated superfluous courses and persuaded teachers to take more subject courses before starting the study of education. The State of California required its high school teaching candidates to have at least a major in one of the subject fields to be taught, plus professional training in education, in order to secure a teaching certificate. College and university professors of traditional subjects, realizing that the schoolmen would welcome their help, interested themselves in the problems of teacher training.[18]

The "egghead," while not exactly a national hero, was, by the middle of President Kennedy's second year in office, accepted by the American public as necessary. Astronaut Scott Carpenter was photographed reading a book while undergoing tests in preparation for his flight.[19]

These and many other manifestations of the public's desire to have a school system dedicated to high scholastic achievement created the demand for good school libraries. Without this demand, the rapid development of school libraries in the 1960's could not have taken place.

---

[17] American Association for the Advancement of Science, *Report on Broad Improvements in Science Teaching* (New York: Science Education News, 1962).

[18] As an example in the shift of the thinking of academic people, the Council on Basic Education *Newsletter* began to emphasize positive accomplishments as well as to point out examples of errors.

[19] Picture on cover of *Library Journal* (July 1962).

CHAPTER V

# The Nature of a School Library
# and Its Elements

The nature of a school library evolves from the nature of the recorded information it contains and from the way such information is to be used in the teaching process.

Even in the smaller schools the school library should be thought of, not as a room, but as a system—a network of services. The use of a library in a school where teaching goes on everywhere in the building cannot be confined to one room. The wisest use involves spreading the services as widely as possible throughout the entire building. But in developing a library system for a school, there are many problems to consider and many mistakes to avoid.

## The Nature of Recorded Information

The process of developing a good system starts with an examination of the nature of recorded information, which may be likened to a series of concentric circles.

The first, or inner circle, called *primary source materials,* consists of the records of the actual events, ideas, or statements, under consideration. A tape-recording of a man's speech would be considered primary source material if all the words come through clearly, whereas a reporter's shorthand notes of the same speech could not be accepted as a true record of the man's statements unless they were verified by two or more reliable witnesses. A newspaper account of a speech is not primary source material because the reporter or the typesetter may have changed the words. The actual handwritten manuscript of a novel or poem would be considered primary source material, whereas a copy of the published edition would not.

The second circle, called *secondary source materials,* consists of published statements written from the primary source materials. A newspaper account of a speech, or of a discussion between two political leaders, would be a secondary source—because at least one intermediary stood between the published story and the actual event.

Textbooks are all secondary sources, even though they may contain accurate photocopies of primary source material. A journal article written by the author of a chemical experiment would contain primary source material, but a story of the experiment, written by a reporter from the published article, would be a secondary source. A government document summarizing ways in which television is used in schools would be a secondary source, but it might cite many primary sources for the information it included.

Failure to distinguish between primary and secondary sources frequently means failure to get at the real facts of the situation. Herein lies the source of much of the misunderstanding that characterizes human relations.

Reference books exist for each field of knowledge. There are so many of these that librarians have compiled printed lists to help them remember what is available. Two such lists are Winchell's *Guide to Reference Books* (1954), with supplements, and Shore's *Basic Reference Sources: An Introduction to Materials and Methods* (1954).

The special professional competence of a skilled librarian lies in her knowledge of reference books. She must know how to use them as keys to unlock the knowledge contained in the world of printed books.

Because these reference books are used as keys to unlock the resources of a library, they are usually kept close to the entrance to the library and to the librarian's office. In helping a student locate information, the librarian works back and forth between the keys, or reference books, and the primary and secondary sources— which constitute the library collection. The reference collection cannot be isolated or separated from the rest of the book collection. To do so would be comparable to putting a telephone directory on one side of the city block and installing the telephone itself on the other side of the block. The two are used interchangeably and need to be kept together.

Failure to understand the interrelationship between the reference collection and the book collection (consisting of primary and secondary sources) led Trump[1] and others to advocate a concept of a library system in which the "central library" consisted of the reference collection while the primary and secondary sources were kept in a series of "learning centers." For the reasons stated above, this division is an impossible one. The schools that tried it found themselves unable to afford the additional staff and duplicate copies of the books that were required.

## The Problem of Centralized Versus Decentralized Libraries

If a school library has sufficient money to provide an adequate library staff in each of its "learning centers," plus duplicate copies of card catalogs and reference books, plus copies of the books that will be needed in each of the centers, the concept of a decentralized library system has many advantages, for the obvious reason that it places the library materials close to the place where the actual teaching is going on. But there would be a few disadvantages, in addition to the costs factor. The student who attempted to locate information on problems that cut across departmental or divisional lines (as most problems do) would be inconvenienced.

All aspects of the centralized-versus-the-decentralized-library problem at the high school level can be analyzed and studied by observing the history of the problem in university libraries, each of which has felt the impact of two forces pulling the library in opposite directions. The fact that all knowledge is interrelated[2] causes practical problems, the solutions to which point to the wisdom of having a centralized library. But because members of the university faculty have to work and teach in buildings apart from the library, they naturally want "their books" near where they work and teach. This would require a decentralized library.

*Relative merits of each.* There are advantages and disadvantages to each system.

A centralized library is more economical in terms of staff and

---

[1] Lloyd Trump, *Images of the Future: A New Approach to Secondary Education* (Urbana, Ill.: Commission on the Experimental Study of the Utilization of the Staff in the Secondary School, 1959).

[2] John P. Mitler, "Social Sciences at Yale," *Yale Graduate School Newsletter* (January 23, 1959).

book costs. Per dollar spent, it can give better reference service and buy more books. It will also be more convenient for students, in that they can come to one building with some assurance that the books they want will be there rather than in one of several departmental libraries.

A decentralized library, while much more expensive to staff and operate, is more convenient for those teachers and students who are working almost exclusively in subject areas in which the library classification numbers bring together in one collection most of the books they want. As is well-known to students of reading behavior,[3] the factor of accessibility is an important stimulant to library use.

But, granted that the problem is important and real at the college and university level, how important is it at the high school level? Is it important that high school students be aware of the interrelation among the various fields of knowledge, or is each field to be studied independently of all others? These are questions to which there are no clear-cut answers; rather, they are questions that involve matters of belief and points of view. Insofar as the schools exist to prepare students to participate in the decision-making process of government, particularly at the local level, it would seem essential for the individual to be able to use, or get at, knowledge in many fields.

There are many ways of demonstrating the extensiveness of the interrelation among different fields of knowledge. The indivisibility of knowledge can be seen by studying the problems man has had in classifying knowledge and in devising classification systems for the carriers of knowledge in libraries. In the nineteenth century, these classification systems worked reasonably well but, by the middle of the twentieth century, they had broken down: most of the books that a library now buys could, with equal justification, fall into more than one category in the classification system.

A second way to perceive the indivisibility of knowledge would be to study the lists of books professors assign to their students for required reading. It will be found that on most of these lists the books are drawn from a half-dozen or more different fields.

A third way would be to look at the books that find their way into those university departmental libraries where no restrictions have

---

[3] Douglas Waples and Ralph Tyler, *What People Want To Read About* (Chicago: The University of Chicago Press, 1931).

been placed on the choice of the faculty. Each departmental library tends to become a miniature, all-inclusive university library with books from many classification areas.

A fourth way would be to watch a library cataloger assign subject headings to the books she adds to the library. For each book she adds, she assigns from three to twenty different subject headings from several branches of knowledge. A study of the cross-references in the Library of Congress *List of Subject Headings* would show the same interrelations.

But, on the other hand, the factor of accessibility is exceedingly important. In a distressingly large number of cases, students and faculty will get along without a book if there is much inconvenience involved in securing it. In large universities, where physical distances are great, the matter of accessibility is so important that decentralized libraries are provided even though they are very costly and are most inconvenient for those who have to go from branch to branch to find their books. These libraries are most useful to the specialist who works in one of the older academic disciplines that has not been affected very much by twentieth-century scientific scholarship.

The problem cannot be resolved easily at the high school level. Most schools have so few books that they cannot adequately support one centralized collection, much less a series of departmental collections.

*A solution.* A solution to the problem of centralized versus decentralized libraries for the schools, regardless of their size, lies in thinking of them as a system, with a strong central library providing various kinds of service to many learning centers throughout the building.

The teachers and the librarian choose from the library collections the books that are appropriate to use, on a temporary basis, in the classrooms, laboratories, or learning centers. These are placed on book trucks and are sent to the place where they are to be used for a given period of time. At the end of that period, they are returned to the library and others are sent out. Collections of this kind can be used at decentralized points without the need for catalogs, reference services, or other expensive elements. The teachers, or others on the team-teaching group, can take care of such matters as charging the books out to readers.

Librarians from the central library can visit these service points frequently to make certain that the collections are being used and that they are meeting the needs of the center.

To serve these learning centers, the central library will need a good photocopying machine, because duplicate copies of journal articles and book pages will be needed. This copying can best be done in the central library.

Under this system, the students and the faculty will not come to place too much reliance on the service collections, as they are almost certain to do with permanent departmental collections. Instead, they know that they must go to the central library for bibliographic and reference books that are not found in the several parts of the library system.

They will also expect to find in the central library the current issues of journals from many fields of knowledge, which they must read if they are to keep up with the new developments in each field. Few library practices cause more inconvenience and anger than the haphazard handling of current issues of journals. Photocopies of articles the faculty want to keep at their desks can be made in the central library.

This method of solving the problem of centralized versus decentralized libraries provides enough of the services the advocates of decentralized learning centers claim for their system without the inconvenience and cost of a departmental library system, and without separating the reference works from the central book collection.

Universities and at least one high school—at West Leyden, Illinois—have developed a library system that combines elements of both the centralized and the decentralized systems. This involves establishing subject divisions within the central library. These divisions are usually labeled *Science, Social Science, Humanities,* and so on. The books are shelved in the division in which the librarian thinks they belong. But because different people will have conflicting ideas about where a given book belongs, the subject-division plan is not an unmixed blessing—particularly if the school had only a small book collection. Furthermore, the plan forces users to rely on the card catalog to find a particular book if its subject is one that might fall in any one of several divisions. The term describing each division may not mean the same thing to all people and does not coincide with the library classification blocks.

But, under certain circumstances (where there is a large, open, undivided floor plan), the subject-division plan can be useful. Most of the worst features of the plan can be minimized if the books are arranged in straight classification order, with each classification block separated from the others in a clearly recognizable manner. This will result in a divisional plan, but each book will be in its normal classification sequence and hence easily found by the students.

## Arrangement of the Elements of a School Library[4]

All libraries, within each type, are arranged on much the same basic plan—not because planners lack imagination, but because the needs of readers in relation to library collections are basically the same.

*The lobby.* At the entrance there is usually some kind of lobby to let one know he is in a library—not in a cafeteria or a physics laboratory or a professor's office—and to create a sound and sight barrier between the library and the rest of the building. The lobby is usually an impressive place and it invites one to explore further.

The lobby usually contains exhibit cases for displays, special shelves for new books, displays of books on special topics that will attract the interest of readers, and chairs to sit on while looking at the exhibits.

The lobby, if it is successful, eases the student into the mood of a library and shows him where he should go to use the rest of the library.

Few school libraries prior to the 1960's were large enough to justify so specialized an area as a lobby. But as collections approached the 50,000-volume level and as seating space for 25–30 per cent of the students became an acceptable idea, the need for such niceties as lobbies and reading lounges became obvious. The schools looked to the experience of college and university libraries for guidance in the arrangement of these areas. One school in particular has won the affection of its students by setting up in the lobby, the last day of classes before each vacation, tables laden with

---

4 Illinois Library Association, *Planning the School Library Quarters* (Chicago: American Library Association, 1950); and H. R. Calvin and K. Devereau, *Proceedings of the Library Buildings Institute,* St. Paul, Minn., June, 1954 (Chicago: American Library Association, 1955).

cookies and coffee for all who enter. Receptions for new members of the faculty, so that they may meet the library staff, are also held there. This concept of a library is a far cry from the old kind of school library typically found in the United States, but it began to be accepted in the junior colleges and high schools in the 1960's.

The lobby display cases are an important part of school library service. Each year there are many traveling exhibits of books that can be had by paying their transportation costs. These exhibits have great appeal for young people. Frequently, these traveling exhibits are made up by foreign governments to show the current output of new books in special fields in their country.

Lobby displays can also be used to help the student see his community as it really is. For example, there could be a series of displays planned around the following topics: The city board of education (with pictures of each board member and an account of what he or she has done, and a chart showing the board's areas of responsibility and activity); industries and important business firms (with pictures, sample products, maps showing the distribution of products, and charts showing financial ratings); the history of the community (with pictures of its founders, accounts of its main events and crises, photographs of principal buildings, and so on); major problems facing the community (with charts stating problems and what is being done about them); the people of the community (with charts showing racial and nationality makeup, pictures of important people, and pictures of clubs, groups, and outstanding leaders). These and other displays would help create a bond of understanding between students and their community.

Displays are a good way of calling attention to all kinds of issues that are important to the students or to issues that the school considers important for the students.

As one goes through the lobby, he should be able to see where the following services in the library are: the charging desk, the library keys (the card catalog and the reference section), and the main stairway (if there is one).

*The charging desk.* Just beyond the door of the lobby should be located the charging desk, in the same area with the keys to the library. Since the charging desk is sometimes the first and last service of the library to be used, it is important that it be close to the lobby. The desk should not face the lobby head-on; it should be placed at right angles to the lobby and to one side, so that the messy housekeeping work associated with the desk will not be visible from the lobby. The area in which the charging desk and the keys are located is a noisy area; hence sound barriers should separate it from the rest of the library.

The size of the charging desk will depend on the size of the school enrollment and the number of charging transactions that are made each day. The librarian and the architect will know how to calculate its proper size. Behind the desk there should be work space for the handling of books that have been returned to the library, as well as space for the books that are kept on closed reserve. This work is best kept out of sight; hence it should be done in a room directly behind the charging desk. The desk itself should be placed about eight feet away from the wall that separates it from the workroom. This distance is necessary to permit the passage of book trucks for books coming back into the library.

The work done at the charging desk is of a kind that can be done by student assistants working under the supervision of the librarian, whose office therefore should be close by.

*The keys (the card catalog and reference center).* The keys to the library consist of the card catalog, bibliographies, reference books, and periodical indexes.

The *card catalog,* the index to the library's books, comes first because it is the key most frequently used. Its size will depend on the number of books in the library: five to six cards per book, eighty cards to an inch of drawer space (not counting index-tab cards), twelve inches per drawer.

About six feet in front of the card catalog there should be a table on which catalog trays may be placed for consultation. The old-fashioned pull-out shelves in the middle of the catalog cabinets should be avoided because they force congestion at the catalog if more than two people are there at the same time.

The periodical indexes, which are indexes to the articles contained in the periodicals the library owns (and in many it does not own), come next. These are multivolume sets, each of which is thick and heavy and requires special kinds of shelving to facilitate its use and preservation. Each school library will have the *Reader's Guide,* while larger libraries will also have the *International Index* and other special subject indexes, such as the *Art Index, Essay and*

*General Literature Index, Public Affairs Information Service, Index to Technical Literature,* and others. Shelves especially designed to hold these indexes are sold by the library supply houses, and are well worth buying because they prolong the physical life of the volumes and facilitate their use.

The reference collection, which consists of books that are special guides to printed information (encyclopedias, bibliographies, directories, handbooks, outlines, dictionaries, atlases, histories, bibliographical directories, and financial services), will vary in size from 300 to 5000 volumes, depending on the wealth of the library, the skill of its staff, and the purposes it serves. A strong reference collection is essential to any school that expects its students to do independent study.

The librarian, who helps readers learn how to use a reference collection, will need a desk near the collections, one at which she can converse in a normal tone of voice without disturbing readers in the rest of the library. She will also need an office in which she can confer at length with individuals and do her own work.

Because reference books are mostly large and heavy, and because one consults rather than reads them, facilities for using them near their shelves should be provided. Furniture that can be used by the reader while standing, as well as ordinary sit-down tables, is essential.

If the collection is small, it can be kept on single-faced wall shelves, but larger collections are best housed in rows of double-faced shelves in ranges, with three three-foot sections to a range. The ranges should be placed six feet apart (measured from center to center). The two bottom and two top shelves of a regular seven-foot-high section should be left unused. The end section on each second range should be only four feet high so that reference books can be placed on top for use. Consultation shelves can also be used for this purpose. They are hung on the stack columns. There should also be tables nearby for readers who need to read and take lengthy notes.

Photocopying services should be available nearby, so that readers can obtain accurate copies of pictures, tables, and charts, as well as of printed statements they wish to use as evidence in papers they may be writing. (This facility, incidentally, helps to discourage the mutilation of library books.)

Special vertical files of pamphlets and other "ephemeral" material—that is, material that goes out of date quickly or that deteriorates without special care—are a normal part of a reference collection, as are maps, globes, atlases, and catalogs of government documents.

Sometimes the current issues of magazines, periodicals, and newspapers are included in the reference collection, but they are not an essential part. Wherever they are, they should be close to lounge-type chairs because most readers like to relax when they are reading a magazine. Reading articles in fat, heavy, bound periodicals is another matter; tables are better for that purpose.

The older practice in school libraries, that of storing back files of periodicals in unbound form in a back room, proved to be too expensive. It forced the library staff members to spend much of their time hunting the unbound issues of periodicals, work which students can do for themselves when the bound volumes are available to them on open shelves. It was found to be cheaper to bind the periodicals and put them out where students could consult them directly. Or, in the case of titles that are seldom used, a microfilm file serves the purpose.

No one has ever found a really satisfactory way of handling current newspapers, some of which are included in most reference collections. The usual practice involves impaling them on split poles and hanging them up as though to dry, but this method pleases no one. Folding each paper once and placing it flat on shelves sounds fine, but unfortunately students sometimes copy their fathers' reading habits, with the result that the library's copies of current newspapers end up on the floor under the tables or in the watercloset, not the place where one expects to find the newspaper.

*The book collections.* The books themselves may be arranged in a wide variety of patterns, on one or more stories or tiers or decks, depending on the size of the library, and the ideas of the librarians and the architects. In the older single-room libraries, the books were kept on shelves around the walls, but for reasons stated earlier and also because only a small collection can be housed in that fashion, the newer libraries store their books in blocks of stack ranges, usually not more than eighteen feet long, and arranged four-and-a-half feet apart (measured between centers of the stack columns). The aisle widths are narrower in this section than in the reference collections because the books themselves are usually smaller. Also, a reader does not usually spend much time reading the books while standing in the aisles; he carries them to a nearby chair.

For convenience in finding books, the blocks of ranges should be placed so that the classification sequence can be followed without forcing readers to thread a maze.

Alternating rows of bookstacks with rows of tables produces unfortunate results. Pursuers of books are a great source of annoyance to readers seated at the tables next to the bookcases. Arranging the ranges in blocks, with easier reader facilities on the far side of the blocks, works better. In fact, the plan of having readers filter through the bookstacks to the reading facilities after they leave the area where the charging desk and keys are kept solves many problems.

The basic plan for arranging the bookshelves will determine the layout of the library, a matter to be decided by the architect and the librarian. The old ideas that the school library had to be on one floor, under the close supervision of the librarian, were abandoned in the 1960's (though not without considerable skepticism on the part of school librarians and administrators). The concept of the school library as a place in which one was supposed to visit and be seen died slowly.

*The readers' facilities.* As was stated earlier, the older school libraries provided very little space for readers, and what space there was lacked privacy, dignity, comfort, and interest. A typical example was the Boulder, Colorado, High School library which, prior to its enlargement in 1964, had 72 seats for an enrollment of 1300.

The newer school libraries are based on the assumptions that many students (as many as 30 per cent of the enrollment) will be in the library from four to six hours per day, that the students differ in age, size, sex, and habits, that they will go to the library for long periods of study, and that they will want to work in many ways from various kinds of learning sources. Some will want to work alone, some in small groups, some will need to talk while working, and some will just want to talk!

The body of a high school student at work is a wondrous thing, full of aches and pains and jerks and spasms and twists and contortions and almost never in complete repose. It demands furniture that is not only sturdy, but varied in shape, size, and kind. (One might wonder if the Creator had studying in mind at all as an expected activity for youth.) When chairs are properly designed, however, readers can sit in them for hours without fatigue or restlessness. Following the introduction of the Steelcase C42 with swept-back legs in the 1950's, chairs that were properly designed for readers became available in wood, steel, and plastic.

Instead of following the older plan of grouping the tables in the center of a rectangular room, the reader facilities in newer libraries are interspaced with blocks of bookstacks, so that the readers may be near the books with which they are working and so that there never appears to be a crowd in any one place. Each area contains not only a few traditional rectangular tables, but also reading-room carrels of several types, occasional and lounge-type chairs, special audiovisual reception booths (with earphones), group-study rooms, conference rooms, motion-picture-viewing rooms for small groups, and possibly a small classroom where an instructor can work on library materials with honors students or other special kinds of classes.

In a newer library, some of the carrels are large enough and well enough equipped to constitute a study center, to which a student is assigned and at which he spends much of his day.[5] Here he can attend some classes via closed-circuit television and here he will use not only books and other traditional library materials but also teaching machines and other so-called programmed learning devices. Perhaps on the shelves would be a collection of basic paperback books for the courses he is attending. He can work from his study center with the kind of library services and materials needed in his independent study program. No longer is it necessary to go to different places for different kinds of carriers of knowledge.

Such study centers are not for all, or even most, students, but only for those that have demonstrated a capacity and willingness to do independent study of good quality. Students working in these centers go to studios and laboratories, as usual, and to their teachers for

---

[5] See examples in Ralph E. Ellsworth and Hobart Wagener, *The School Library* (New York: Educational Facilities Laboratory, Inc., 1963), and in Educational Facilities Laboratories, Inc., *Study Carrels—Designs for Independent Study Space* (Stanford: The School Planning Laboratory, Stanford University, 1963).

guidance and direction. Gruber's[6] University of Colorado Behavior Research Laboratory Report No. 19, a study of the reaction of college-level students to this concept, indicates its value when used properly. Files of *The Independent Student* offer evidence of honors programs at the high school level that are clearly far more complex and advanced than public schools had thought possible prior to the 1960's. Likewise, experiments exhibited in science fairs show clearly that high school students are capable of creative work of a high caliber when properly taught and when allowed to work with good facilities.

The newer libraries provide seating space for 20–30 per cent of the student body, instead of the 5 per cent that was common prior to 1950. Because the students spend more of their day in the library and less in the classroom, the over-all size of the school building has not increased, but the library occupies a larger percentage of the total floor space.

The layout of these libraries has to be planned to accommodate the movement of many students without disturbing other readers. The problem is comparable to one that has been faced by college libraries, and consequently the experience gained by college libraries has been followed. The influence of such institutions as Foothills Junior College and Stephens College was widespread.

One basic solution to the handling of large numbers of readers in a library is to bring the students into the reading areas through an aisle, on either side of which are rows of bookstacks placed at right angles to the aisles—within, of course, the lobby and keys area. The result achieved by this method is that students come into the library to find out from the library keys and staff what books they want, and then they go to the shelves for their books and on through the stacks to the study spaces. Much of the noise and confusion of the traffic is absorbed by the keys area, the central aisle, and the stacks.

A second method, mentioned earlier, is to divide the area, checkerboard fashion, into alternate blocks of bookstacks and reading facilities. The need for supervision, so necessary in the older libraries, disappears in these libraries, as it had in the college libraries a

6 H. E. Gruber and Morris Weitman, *Self-Directed Work Experiments in Higher Education.* University of Colorado Behavior Research Report 19, Boulder, Colo., April 1962.

decade before, because they are planned as places in which a student studies, not as places where he visits with his friends or attempts to outsmart the study-hall supervisor. The small percentage of incorrigible students is not allowed to spoil the opportunity of the large majority to have the kind of study facilities they need to permit them to do their best work. The recognition that majorities, too, have rights, helps solve the problem of what to do with unruly minorities.

One of the great advantages of the printed book as a learning medium is that the reader can pick it up and start using it without having to resort to machines. He can glance through it and see if it meets his needs. He can browse among the books without involving other people or machines. Therefore, it is important that books in a school library be kept on open shelves. Most audiovisual materials, on the other hand, cannot be used in this manner. A film has to be taken to a projector and used with the machine. So with slides, tapes, phonograph records, and the like. The materials themselves have no "personality," as a book does. The person who wants to "browse" through a collection of audiovisual materials must do so through some kind of catalog. Thus there is no point in providing direct access to audiovisual materials. They can be kept in a storage room behind the charging desk, where temperature and humidity conditions can be controlled.

Readers find, in the carrels, electrical outlets into which they can plug the teaching machines borrowed at the library charging desk. Tapes for these machines are sold or distributed free at the desk or by the teachers.

Exhibits for programmed learning, a new development of the early 1960's, constitute a regular part of the reading rooms of the school library. They are placed there, under the supervision of a specialist, rather than in another part of the school building, so that students can work back and forth between them and the books and other study materials in the library. These exhibits take many forms. Some, like the dioramas in a museum, are used to teach subjects which involve things, places, people, and other physical properties. Some, in the form of a one-man viewing station, offer an illustrated lecture on a specific topic or problem.

Because these exhibits take up floor space, involve expensive machinery and equipment, are costly to develop and keep up to date, and because too little is known about which subjects are best taught through such devices rather than through books, their adoption has been slow. But because of the advantages they offer for teaching subjects that do not involve ideas and abstract concepts, where language has to be involved, it is assumed that their use will increase steadily. Because the language of thought is the alphabet, the word, and the mathematical symbol, and because these are most efficiently and economically presented in printed form, the book has continued to be used for the teaching of many subjects, particularly those for which thinking and reasoning are essential elements.

The school library has continued to be in a constant state of readjustment as the carriers of information assume new forms.

*Staff workrooms.* Somewhere near the entrance to the library there needs to be a series of workrooms for the staff. Immediately behind the charging desk there should be a circulation desk workroom, where books and portable audiovisual equipment and materials can be handled while they are being discharged and sent to their storage place. Tapes for teaching machines as well as phonograph records would be kept there, along with other information carriers which are appropriately kept somewhere other than in the reading rooms.

There should also be two kinds of offices for the library staff.

The assemblying room is a room in which librarians and teachers meet to work together on library problems. The specific work that is done here includes:

1. Selection of books and other materials that are to be bought for the library. This involves working from publishers' catalogs, booksellers' catalogs, bibliographies, book reviews, and other similar sources of information. It results in joint decisions on books to be purchased.
2. Selection of books that are to be discarded from the library. The librarian will have brought into the rooms, on book trucks, the books she thinks should be discarded. The teachers review the librarian's suggestions and joint final decisions are made. The books are then either returned to the shelves, put in the trash cans, or disposed of in other ways.
3. Selection of the books that are to be sent, on a temporary basis, to the classrooms, laboratories, studios, or learning centers. The librarian and teachers may work from lists, or they may go, with a book truck, to the book shelves and make their choice there. The librarian may have assembled a book truck of materials from which final choices are made by the teachers. After final

decisions have been made, the books are charged out at the desk and are sent to their destination.

4. Inspection of newly published books brought by publishers' representatives or local bookstore dealers for possible purchase. The librarian asks the appropriate teacher to come and help make the choice.

5. Inspection and evaluation of audiovisual materials by the staff, the audiovisual specialists, and the teachers.

6. Preparation and assembly of exhibits.

These rooms did not exist in the older libraries because the library was not thought of as a system and therefore activities carried on in these rooms were not a normal part of library work. In the large cities these activities were sometimes carried on by the school library supervisor in the administrative center. The lack of such rooms and activities in school libraries was evidence of the way in which the library and the librarians were isolated from the teaching process.

In the *technical processes room,* the ordering, classifying, and cataloging work is done. Here also books are labeled, repaired, and sent to and from the library. This room should be adjacent to the librarian's office because she, or someone on her professional staff, will work in the room, at least to supervise the work that is done there by others. It should be emphasized, again, that a centralized cataloging service is available in several forms, for all or most of the books and materials a school library acquires and that those services free the librarian for other work. During the 1950's and 1960's, school librarians especially in the smaller schools, had considerable difficulty realizing that they really could buy their books precataloged. Some seemed to cling to cataloging as a refuge from the kind of relationships that are essential in the teaching process. They had not been trained to develop such relationships and they had had, in the past, no way of getting out from under the cataloging work.

## Control Points

Although universities and research libraries find it necessary to inspect, at the library's exit, the books taken from the library to make certain that charge records have been made, school libraries do not ordinarily find this necessary. When their book collections become large, however, and when it becomes impossible to maintain a high level of student responsibility, some kind of exit control may be necessary. This should be taken into consideration at the time the library is planned. If the library is located within the building, so that several exits are provided, thought should be given to the possibility of closing all but one if controls become necessary. In small libraries, the exit inspection can be combined with the charging-desk operations, but in larger libraries the charging-desk attendants will be too busy to do the exit checking.

In schools that emphasize independent study, students will need to use the school library in the evenings and on weekends. This means that the school may need to keep the library open at times when the rest of the building is closed. To avoid problems of having students (and nonstudents) wandering through unsupervised parts of the building, the library entrance should be close to an entrance to the building, or at least arrangements should be made so that corridors can be blocked off, thus restricting the movements of students to supervised areas. This need may be in direct conflict with the need for having the library in a central position in the school. The choice of location will depend on the layout of the building.

# CHAPTER VI

# The Physical Aspects of a School Library

## Problems

In most public high schools prior to 1960 the library occupied little space and was considered an unimportant part of the school program. Little attention was given to it by architects and planners and its arrangement tended to be highly standardized. But a library, as a cultural institution, symbolizes the power of knowledge and learning. It is therefore given a place of high honor in those cultures that hold learning in high respect. It was natural that in the post-Sputnik years the schools should emphasize the library as a learning center and should give it the kind of architectural significance its role would suggest. The lack of stereotyped architectural expression, characteristic of the newer school libraries, reflects the wide variety of programs recently developed to meet the needs of the rapidly changing American society.

At first, planners had difficulty persuading the community of the necessity for providing space to house a collection of 30,000 to 50,000 volumes and to provide study space for 20–30 per cent of the enrollment. It was frequently necessary to start with a smaller library unit and to expand it gradually. To do this, the libraries were located within the school buildings in areas[1] that could subsequently be expanded. There were several ways of accomplishing this.

The library could be so planned that one wall was an exterior wall of the building that could, at a later date, be removed to permit the library to grow externally into new space, not into space already used for other purposes.

In one-story buildings interior courts were sometimes provided, on the assumption that at a later date they would be filled in and occupied as part of the library. This plan sometimes encountered

---

[1] Ralph E. Ellsworth and Hobart Wagener, *The School Library* (New York: Educational Facilities Laboratories, Inc., 1963).

difficulties if the courts were beautiful and much beloved by the school. No one wanted to give them up.

A third plan frequently used was to locate classrooms, study halls, and other large open areas adjacent to the first unit of the library. At a later time, the partitions between the two areas were removed and thus new space was found for the library. The invaded functions were then moved into space that could be financed more easily than library space. There is a kind of inescapability about providing classroom space that frequently does not apply to libraries.

A fourth idea was to plan the original building so that the upper floors of the library could be used at first for classrooms and other functions and then released to the library as needed. It was necessary, when this idea was used, to plan the location of stairwells and elevators so that the completed library could be operated efficiently.

A fifth plan was to start branches of the library for specific subject areas as the need arose.

A sixth plan, particularly appropriate when a new wing was being added to an existing building, was to locate the library at the junction of the original building and the new wing, but in such a way that it could be enlarged independently of the rest of the structure.

A seventh plan, used only in large school systems, was to give the library a structure of its own that could be enlarged in units as the library grew. Several British, and a few American, private schools possess five separate library buildings but, at the time of this writing, the author knows of no public secondary school in this country that has been able to provide this kind of facility.[2]

Schools that could anticipate, at the time a new building was constructed, an enrollment ceiling and that could provide seating space for 25–30 per cent of this enrollment, would face only the additional problem of finding space for an ever-growing book collection. One way to solve this problem when new space was not available was to spread out the original bookstacks and then, as the collection grew, to move them closer together. A second method, one that seldom worked, was to try to hold the collection to a specified size and to discard old books as new ones were added. A third method was to build the periodicals collection in microfilm form instead of in bound volumes.

---

[2]Anthony Thompson, *Library Buildings in Britain and Europe* (London: Butterworth & Co. [Publishers], Ltd., 1963), pp. 215, 217, 219, 222.

A fourth plan, the one traditionally adopted by colleges and universities, was to accept the idea that a growing book collection was a source of great pride to the college and to the community and to make the task of finding new space for its growth, not a disagreeable burden, but an opportunity to add to the wealth of the school.

A fifth plan was to work out cooperative storage plans with the city or county public library. One of the ill-defined areas of community library development that has existed since the turn of the century has been the provision of library service to young people by both the public and school library. Progress on this problem received new impetus when the American Library Association, at its 1963 annual convention, devoted an entire three-day convention-within-a-convention to the problem of concentrating all community library services to meet the needs of the schools. This was followed by closer coordination between public and school libraries in many cities.

Homemakers and schoolchildren constitute the two largest groups of users of the public library.[3] A question has been raised: Why need there be two libraries, each giving service to schoolchildren? In the larger cities, a sensible division of labor has been worked out, but the problem has by no means been solved, particularly in the smaller communities. A new spirit of cooperation, however, began to prevail after 1963, and the public librarians welcomed the opportunity to supplement the school library's collection of study materials for students, many of whom would later become, as adults, patrons of the public library.

Where this spirit prevailed, the school librarian felt free to count on the public library for financial support. In the larger cities the public library book collection was strong enough to carry much of the burden of providing materials for special school papers and projects.

Other libraries, such as county libraries and the state libraries in some states, provided lending collections and special services to school libraries. None of these outside services, however, could be extensive enough to substitute for a strong library in each school, where the students spend their days.

---

[3] See various studies by Waples, Burleson, and Carnovsky at the University of Chicago.

## The Architectural Character
## of a School Library

Architectural quality, or character, is hard to define but easy to recognize when it exists. A building has architectural character when it is completely appropriate to its function; when it reveals a tasteful and interesting use of line, mass, proportion, and material; when it is full of happy space surprises, when it makes the viewer's heart "leap up for joy." Occasionally a building, like a person, may have a fine character, but may still be hard to live with in small ways.

School libraries with fine architectural character began to appear in the 1960's, but prior to that time there were many among other types of libraries. A few examples would include: (1) the storytelling amphitheaters in the Midland, Michigan, Public Library and in the Kansas City Public Library; (2) the sculptured quality of the Mount St. Scholastica library in Atchison, Kansas; (3) the exposed concrete structural harmonies in the Colorado College library; (4) the warmth of design in the Washington University library; (5) the sensible usability in the Harvard University Lamont Library; (6) and the dramatic daring quality of the Beineke Rare Book Library at Yale. Dozens could be cited. But in the public schools, in the 1950's and the 1960's, architects had considerable difficulty breaking through community resistance against what were considered "architectural frills." Even so sensible a facility as carpeting was installed only after much argument. The public accepted new architectural design and elegance in bars, banks, department stores, filling stations, colleges, and universities, but not in school libraries. The experience Hobart Wagener, an architect, had in trying to provide an interesting school library in Boulder, Colorado, in 1963 was typical.

The red-brick, square, three-story public school buildings in use throughout the Midwest and the West at the turn of the century seem, in retrospect, a perfect expression for the kind of education that prevailed then, even though the style has since lost its appeal. Today, the school buildings erected during the 1920's and 1930's seem fussy and characterless, even though they seemed right to the people who built them. The low, spread-out ranch-house style of the 1960's may seem strange by the year 2000. It may even be that the glass walls intended to invite the outside in may lead another generation to wonder if Nature isn't better left outside. H. H. Richardson seemed as appropriate to his time as Yamasaki does to his. But, in spite of this, there is considerable truth in the claim that architects in the 1960's were allowed by the public, for the first time, to infuse their buildings with a grace, nonfunctional in nature, not to be found in the older buildings. It is also true that the wide diversity of the school programs in the 1960's almost demanded the kind of architectural expression one finds in the newer schools of this period. And, noteworthy, too, is the fact that the most famous architects interested themselves in school buildings.

As long as the concept of the school library was restricted to a one-room rectangle, there wasn't much challenge for an architect. But the larger concept, as described here, gave architects an opportunity to apply their best creative efforts. School libraries began to acquire a special character of their own.

There arose conflicts of interest that were hard to reconcile. For instance, the rapidly changing nature of the school programs and methods in the 1960's, as well as the rapidly growing population, almost demanded that the architect use a loft, or modular, type of construction that could be adapted, remodeled, and enlarged at low cost and without interfering too much with the school session. But it was difficult to give a loft, or modular, building the desired element of surprise or gracefulness. How could the architect give character to the form?

## The Special Architectural Needs
### of a School Library

*Lighting.* Except in reading areas along the north wall of a library, natural sunlight cannot be used satisfactorily as a source of light, because it will be either too bright or too dim, depending on weather conditions, and it cannot penetrate far enough into the room to do much good.

Very little is known about what constitutes good reading light in spite of the fact that many so-called authorities write as though there was real scientific evidence to back up their generalizations. Nevertheless, the following simple guidelines are reasonably safe:[4]

---

[4] Keyes D. Metcalf, "Lighting," in forthcoming book on college and university library buildings, to be published by McGraw-Hill Book Company in 1965 and *Light and Vision,* University of Michigan Continued Education Series No. 76 (Ann Arbor: University of Michigan, 1958).

1. Glare from sunlight or bright light is unpleasant and painful.[5]
2. High degrees of color contrast on surfaces that are in the line of vision cause eyestrain.
3. There is little reason, for ordinary reading, for light levels that exceed 50 foot-candles. In areas where one must consult catalogs and books with fine print, up to 75 or even 100 foot-candles are helpful.
4. Unhappiness with a lighting installation is probably caused less by low light levels than by improper light sources, high degrees of color contrast, glare, and other less visible sources of discomfort (such as high temperatures and stale air).

*Ventilation and temperature.* During the 1960's parents frequently remarked about the overheated conditions they found in the classrooms when they returned for Parents' Night or PTA meetings. The author has visited nearly a hundred schools and has found overheated rooms in most of the buildings. Why should this be so when it is known that children neither need nor like the high temperatures older people prefer? Perhaps the thermometers are set to please the teachers and administration.

Also, few schools have been able to afford to spend the money necessary to get good automatically controlled ventilation systems. In buildings that are inadequately air conditioned, people become angry when they cannot open the windows. But when they can open them, their feeling of relief is probably only psychological, because what they are actually doing is weakening an already weak system.

Most high school students are comfortable reading in temperatures that range from 70° to 74° and in rooms in which there is enough air circulation so that one is unaware of the quality of the air. It is believed that most people are comfortable when the humidity level is between 35 and 45 per cent. It is known that most people are uncomfortable when the air around them is stagnant, regardless of its temperature. It is believed that older people like higher temperatures than young people do. Ventilation systems that provide thermostats in each room seem to invite control by persons who like high temperatures, and these are likely to be the teachers, not the students—simply on the basis of age differences.

In libraries, the situation is a similar one. A physically inactive librarian sets the thermostats to suit her needs, usually not realizing that the students might like a different temperature range.

---

[5] Henry Logan, "Lighting Libraries," *Library Journal,* (1952), 2128–29.

*Sound levels.* The extremes of the tomb-like silence associated with libraries in the past and the roar in the undisciplined school libraries of the 1930's and 1940's obviously are both to be avoided. The most desirable situation seems to be one in which a pleasant sound level made up of undistracting noises (e.g., air coming out of a ventilation duct) is high enough to mask out the noises that *are* distracting to readers (such as the clatter of high heels on a hard surface, the chatter of a typewriter, the roar of a motor bike, the talk of a librarian, the pop of bubble gum). Because people differ in their reactions to sound levels, there should be special places—for instance, in the carrels and study centers—where there is less noise, and other places—for instance, in group-study rooms—where more noise is tolerable.

In addition to the customary application of sound-deadening materials to ceilings, the use of carpeting in libraries has proved to be useful in keeping sound levels where they should be, without the necessity of an imposed silence.

*Furniture.* There should be a wide variety of kinds and sizes of furniture. Some three-fourths of the regular study space should be in the form of reading-room carrels, that is, table space three feet wide and two feet deep, with sixteen-inch tall baffles or dividers on three sides, giving the reader visual privacy on three sides.[6] Some flat-top tables should be provided for readers who like to spread out their maps and papers. Lounge-type chairs should be of several types and sizes to match the needs of the individual readers. Single lounge chairs rather than davenports are helpful deterrents to the temptation of Morpheus, not to mention Eros.

Such facilities would present problems in the larger city school systems, in which a minority of incorrigible students sometimes creates behavior problems of a serious nature. Such schools have had to forego the privilege of having first-rate study facilities. On the other hand, school librarians and administrators have frequently made the mistake of assuming that most high school students require close supervision when, in reality, their bad behavior has only been a normal response to an unpleasant and improper library environment.

---

6 "Student Reactions to Study Facilities . . ." A Report to the Presidents of Amherst, Mount Holyoke, Smith College, and the University of Massachusetts. The Committee for New College, Amherst, Mass., 1960.

# CHAPTER VII

# The Program—The Library as
# a Learning Instrument

## A Point of View

Just as it can be said that an individual achieves happiness, not by seeking it deliberately, but by living properly, so it can be said that a school's ability to graduate students with good reading habits comes, not as a result of special reading-promotion projects, but as the result of good teaching. Even so, there is a block of student time that will be spent under the influence of the forces that reach him outside the instructional program of the school. The library can, in its own right, have some influence on student reading behavior, if it will do those things that give a library personality and that penetrate deeply enough to capture the student's attention, interest, and enthusiasm.

The recommendations that have been made in this volume would, if adopted, provide the point of view, the procedures, and the physical conditions to make the library function properly as part of the school's teaching program. They also provide the basis upon which an appropriate program of reading stimulation might be built. Once the fundamentals have been provided, the rest depends much on the ability of the librarian to dramatize the values of reading so vividly that the students will be influenced into reading habits and practices which they might otherwise not have known.

The ones reached are likely to become the honors students of the college they attend, if they go to college. Although a study published in 1963[1] showed that there was little relationship between good high school library facilities and the academic success of students (measured by grade point average) in lower-division-level courses in college, this fact is not in contradiction to the preceding statement. The

---

[1] R. D. Walker, *The Availability of Library Service and Academic Achievement,* (Chicago: research series, No. 4: Springfield, Illinois State Library, 1963), p. 51.

kind of achievement that results from becoming a good reader is not likely to become involved until upper-division college work is undertaken.

The forces competing for the students' time are strong and attractive, but behind the library is a long line of great personalities—Moses, Homer, Jesus, Augustine, Dante, Shakespeare, Darwin, Einstein, Camus. Each has something important to say. Each one has wrestled with the same basic problems that torment high school seniors today. Each has something worthwhile to contribute to the solution of these problems.

## What Can a Librarian Do to Help Students Become Good Readers?

First, the librarian herself must be distinguished in personality, education, training, and knowledge of books, so that she may win the respect and attention of the faculty. If the teachers are proud of "their" librarian and the work she is doing, they will convey their enthusiasm to their students, and they will go out of their way to create in the students a sense of pride in the library. This is the first requirement and on it are based all the other factors for success.

Second, the librarian must be so genuinely and naturally interested in books that her interest radiates to others. This interest cannot be faked or imposed; it has to be a true outer manifestation of an inner intellectual curiosity.

Third, the librarian should be wise in the ways of teen-agers, and she must be so approachable that students will go to her with their reading problems. As all schoolmen and parents know, high school students are full of problems and worries, and they crave an opportunity to talk out their problems with adults with whom they feel at ease—even though they frequently do not know how to get the conversation started. The librarian is in a unique position to be helpful because her response to questions can be indirect, in the guise of a recommendation of a book in which the characters may have something to say on the problem that is troubling the student. To make effective and relevant recommendations, she must have stored away in her memory the contents of great books, the characters in which do battle with important problems. Their struggles help the reader to project himself into their situations. The essential versimilitude of great literature, as tested by generation after generation of readers, constitutes the main reason that students find these great books helpful—even though the style of writing may be strange and the setting unfamiliar.

Because they must know the contents of the world's great books, librarians should have a full and undiluted liberal arts education before they begin their technical training. Knowledge of the arts of teaching and of librarianship is helpful, but it cannot substitute for a knowledge of the contents of great books.

Fourth, the position of the librarian should be established by the school administration as an academic teaching position, as a part of the instructional program of the school. This relationship, if the librarian is capable of living up to it, will enable her to work as part of the teaching team in the planning of courses. The administration should make it clear to the teaching staff members that their plans for teaching should be coordinated with the librarian well in advance.

### What a Librarian Does—in Detail

The librarian expects to make a major part of her contribution through the teachers. She helps them to select and to assemble in the library the best possible teaching materials, including audiovisual aids. She encourages the teachers to recommend good books to students. She brings to the teachers' attention books that might not be known to them. She sees to it that in each classroom there is a book truck of library materials to supplement the teacher's work. She enlists the help of the teachers in selecting new books for purchase. She studies the way in which students in each class study; if she can learn from her observations anything that might help the teacher improve her use of library materials, she talks it over with the teacher.

Although the point seems not to be well understood by school administrators, it should be remembered that although the teacher knows a great deal about the subject content of her field of knowledge, her knowledge of relevant books and audiovisual materials will usually be limited. This will be particularly true when the teacher is teaching subjects in which her college preparation was not strong. But teachers will also need help (as librarians can testify from actual experience) in keeping up with the new materials in the fields in which they have specialized. Librarians, on the other hand, have been trained to know how to use bibliographic tools to locate relevant materials in all fields. Librarians cannot be expected to be subject experts—at least not in more than one subject field, but they can use their knowledge of bibliographies and other sources to supplement the knowledge of the classroom teacher.

The librarian arranges the library so that it is physically attractive. She administers it so that rules do not stand in the way of the reader's enjoyment. She develops displays to attract the attention of students and to arouse their curiosity to the point where they want to read more about the subject. Realizing that a library is a center for all the arts, the librarian will see to it that paintings and pieces of sculpture are included in the library, as well as a large collection of phonograph records of orchestral and vocal music.

The librarian will keep restrictive rules to a minimum and will try to have just one policy: to meet the needs of each individual as he or she states them, unless doing so interferes with the rights of other readers. "Thou shalt not" signs should not be used, or signs that command "Silence." There will be, for those who prefer them, reading areas where silence is maintained both by rule and by proper physical environment.

The librarian will offer photocopying services at the charging desk to expedite the use of library materials that should not be taken from the library—such as reference books, and the like.

The librarian will see that a library club is organized for those students who are particularly interested in books and libraries or in librarianship as a career. She will try to encourage the habit of book collecting, particularly of the kind of local records that are so frequently destroyed and that later prover to be so useful to historical researchers. Teachers might encourage students to try to spot young, potentially creative people and to collect evidence of their creativity before they become famous. Even if nothing comes of 95 per cent of the attempts, the rewards of the remaining 5 per cent will be rich.

The librarian will try to be available to talk with students in the library at the time of day when most students would be likely to go to her for reading counseling. She will cultivate the reputation of being willing to help students with their problems in locating materials for study or report writing.

She will appreciate the fact that the school administrators do not have the time to search out the materials they would like to read, even if they know of their existence. The librarian will watch for this type of material and will place it on the desk of the administrator.

She works closely with the librarians, of the city library, the college library (if there is one in town), and of the state library, from whom she will be borrowing books.

The librarian works closely with the audiovisual specialist in the school so that all kinds of learning sources will be equally available to the individual reader in the library.

She organizes her work so that she has time to read extensively. Her reading is her homework.

She will try to build her staff of professional librarians so that each one will be a specialist in a given subject area and so that, collectively, they have an acquaintance with books in all fields of knowledge.

She will supervise the staff of student workers, on the assumption that they can learn a great deal from their work in the library. They are not just paid employees: few people who handle books can resist the temptation of finding out what's inside them!

She will maintain in the library, preferably in the lobby, special display shelves of new books on topics of current interest to the students, and she will be wise in choosing topics that will attract the interest of students. To do this, the librarian herself must be keenly aware of what is happening to contemporary society and what students are thinking about. An ivory-tower point of view is not appropriate in a school librarian.

## The Book Collection and the Library Program

The book collection is, of course, the essence of the school library. There were many reasons why school libraries, prior to the 1960's, had very few books and a perpetual shortage of funds. These reasons have been discussed earlier in this volume. They reside in the attitudes of the American public, the boards of education, and the school administrators toward the basic purposes of the school system and toward methods of teaching. These attitudes began to shift in the post-World War II period toward greater emphasis on traditional scholarship and toward the placing of more responsibility on the student himself for the progress he might make. During the transition period, there was much futile and frustrating discussion of the "disciplines" versus the "life adjustment" basis for education, and very little clarification of issues resulted. Nevertheless, the public schools did begin to shift their emphasis in such a way as to make large libraries essential.

In part, the change was a matter of stepping up the pace, of emphasizing quality, of stressing independent study, of introducing honors programs that involved wide reading, and of toughening up the workload of students. At the same time, this period gave professional educators a chance to put into practice many of the new ideas that they, in cooperation with subject specialists, had been studying. For example, new ways of teaching foreign languages, the biological sciences, and physics all produced observable results. Postwar problems created a public consciousness that was reflected in intensified study of governmental, economic, political, and social issues. Because so many of these problems had to be studied from new points of view, with new methodologies and intellectual tools, the textbooks had to be supplemented with large libraries, with collections sufficiently rich and varied to permit students to work on problems in some depth.

Here the problem of school size was critical. The small community was unable to afford a high school book collection of 50,000 volumes (or 30,000 volumes if a good public library was accessible to the students). Because the number of books a school should have depends so much on the factors discussed earlier, it was inevitable that there was little uniformity from school to school. In the stronger schools, where there was an emphasis on independent study, the 30,000–50,000-volume standard was basic—in the sense that a library had to have that many books to sustain reasonable searches in the kinds of problems high school students wished to tackle. Adults in this era had difficulty in believing that students were capable of handling the kinds of problems they tried to tackle, but in this they were recalling what they—the parents—were like in their high school years. They were failing to see the world as it looks to high school students of today. The difference was so great that it could be said truthfully that high school students in the 1960's were working at levels that were common in the colleges in the 1920's.

The problem of convincing the communities that the money required to buy and support an adequate school library was a reasonable expenditure was largely a matter of getting them to see the problem in proper perspective. The public had come to accept the cost of large gymnasiums, coaching staffs for football, basketball, and baseball, well-drilled and elaborately outfitted bands, well-equipped workshops for vocational-training programs, and good laboratories for science programs. Art studios were found in many schools. Money seemed to be available for everything except the single most important tool essential to the development of the student mind—books. Once the public realized the lack of balance in its attitude, the error began to be corrected.

There were controversial issues involved. For example, the question of whether it is wise to permit or encourage high school students to read about any problem in depth was debated. Might this not interfere with the students' acquiring a balanced summary of all fields of knowledge?

Also, there was the question of scope of the school program. Contrary to what the public thought, the number of subjects, or fields of knowledge, that must be covered in a high school was not a matter that could be decided arbitrarily by the teachers, the school administration, or even by the school board. Fundamentally, this is a matter that is determined by the number and nature of the problems that face a society, and that seem to make up the world for which the schools are trying to prepare the students. In the nineteenth century, the number of these problems was small; in the first half of the twentieth century, it grew at a fantastic rate.

The argument that the schools could not enlarge the scope and content of their curriculums because students could not enlarge their capacity to absorb information without developing neuroses, was answered in two ways: first by the fact that during the last three thousand years, man has shown that he could expand the capacity of his mind as widely as he wished; and second, by the findings of psychologists and anthropologists, which indicate that man has not yet learned to think with more than a small part of his brain capacity.

At the time of this writing, there are no adequate published guides listing the books which should be in a high school library of 50,000 —or even 30,000—volumes. Existing guides have assumed that collections of 5000–8000 volumes are enough. The closest approximation is the printed list, *Basic Books for Junior College Libraries: 20,000 Vital Titles*.[2] But this list was compiled for junior colleges, not high schools. *Three Thousand Books for Secondary School Libraries*,[3] issued by the Independent Schools Education Board, though of limited scope, would be directly useful.

## The Library Program and the Changing Curriculum

The problem of expanding and revising the subject content of the curriculum has had unusual relevance in the second half of the twentieth century. Not only is there so much new knowledge to absorb for its own sake, but man's ability to solve the governmental problems facing him (in those parts of the world which follow the ideal of democracy) depends on the ability of his leaders to win approval for new proposals that must necessarily depart sharply from old traditions and assumptions. These proposals cannot win approval unless the public understands. But the public cannot understand unless the public knows.

For example, on the continent of Africa there have been racial conflicts along with the clashes resulting from the quest for independence. Until the mid-1950's these could be viewed by the average American as serious and important problems for the Africans, and possibly for the Europeans who had colonies in Africa, but not as problems that might affect his own economic well-being or his personal safety. But by 1960, it had become evident that unless there was general understanding about the problems of each of the new nation-states, the public could not tell whether or not its government was handling its policies in Africa wisely. And on that question—that is to say, foreign relations—the Presidential elections of 1960 turned.

The amount of information the citizen had to have about the laws of economic behavior was relatively small until the 1960's, when choices had to be made on such problems as the importation of cheap foreign goods, and the degree to which the federal government could or should control the economy.

---

[2] Charles L. Trinkner, *Basic Books for Junior College Libraries: 20,000 Vital Titles* (Northport, Ala.: Colonial Press, 1963).

[3] *Independent Schools Education Board, Three Thousand Books for Secondary School Libraries* (New York: R. R. Bowker Co., 1961).

Nor could the taxpayers of the 1960's evaluate the wisdom of expending large sums of money on space exploration, unless they knew enough about science and research to calculate the possible returns on such efforts, enough about military history to calculate its risks, or enough about human history to know what has happened before when people have faced comparable problems.

The secondary school system in the second half of the twentieth century, in short, found that universal education carried with it the obligation of teaching everyone more knowledge than the experts of previous generations had had to master. The stakes involved the survival of the ideals of the Western world. The solution to this problem was sought in several ways: (1) by increasing the amount of information taught in the schools; (2) by improving the methods of teaching; (3) by extending the school system to thirteen or even fourteen years through the organization of community colleges; (4) by making attendance in the community colleges almost universal; and (5) by introducing various forms of adult education.

Because one of the peculiar problems involved was that of under-.standing what might be called the psychology of peoples—peoples whose cultures were different from that of Americans—the literature of imagination as well as the literature of power was needed. Urgently needed were examples of the novels, poetry, plays, musical compositions, dances, and art that traditionally have provided the windows through which one can look into people's minds. Also needed was all the factual information available.

Scholarly techniques that have yielded understanding of how and why other peoples think and act the way they do—such as cross-cultural anthropological surveys—became useful in the schools. Reports of explorations by missionaries, doctors, hunters, and philosophers were sought for the shelves of school libraries. Reference books, such as gazeteers, statistical handbooks, and other guides to the accumulated knowledge about the world were also needed in the school libraries.

The pace of learning suddenly stepped up from a mild concern with problems of reading readiness and "life adjustment" to a sober realization that in a time of crisis everyone has to be ready and that the adjustments that have to be made are between cultures, not just between the individual and his own culture.

But the scope of school libraries had to be expanded—not just to include books by and about all the peoples of the world, but also to provide the information needed to meet changes in the American Society that have resulted from the advances of technology. Technology was providing machines that did manual and physical work and thus created unemployment among unskilled groups. At the same time it was creating many more new jobs at the managerial, highly technical,[4] and professional levels than the schools and colleges could turn out graduates to fill. The effects of these changes forced the schools to pay less attention to the less able students and to provide more attention and facilities for the more able. This required more books and journals of an advanced nature in the school libraries, which came more nearly to resemble the college libraries of the prewar years than the high school libraries of that period.

Fear that high school students could not handle this complex knowledge had been largely dispelled by the experience with accelerated programs for able students started during World War II, and by the experiences of the schools that started the new programs. The following paragraph from a newspaper account of a National Education Association survey of current practices states the case very well:

> If a trend could be spotted among the seventy districts which replied to the NEA inquiry, it might be that some districts are adopting courses in humanities and world culture which are usually thought of as being at the college level. Scarsdale, New York; Mount Lebanon, Pennsylvania; Beachwood, Ohio; Riverside, Illinois; and University City, Mississippi, were among the communities which reported introduction of such courses. Lake Forest, Illinois, reported a new course in logic, surely a college-level subject. Only Grosse Point, Michigan, among these communities reported nothing particularly new this year, but Grosse Point was pretty well advanced to begin with.[5]

In short, all kinds of pressures—community, state, national, and international—forced the public schools to place greater emphasis on the teaching of learning skills and habits so that students could achieve greater capacity for learning on an independent basis. These

---

[4] John Fischer, "The Stupidity Problem," *Harper's Magazine* (September 1962), 14–24.

[5] Wealthy Suburbs Set Pace in Educational Innovation" (Washington, D.C.: National Education Association, 1962).

pressures also caused the schools to increase the traditionally difficult and scientific subject content of the curriculum and to interna-
tionalize the scope of their courses. And all these changes required
school libraries of considerable size.

# CHAPTER VIII

# The School Library and
# Community Relations

The typical American community has been almost unaware of the school library, at least not to the extent that it has been aware of the school band, the vocational-education shops, the home economics facilities, or the athletic teams. About the only school library problem that has reached the public's attention is that involved in the question of censorship and labeling. This issue has taken two forms: the refusal of the school administration or the librarian to buy for the school library books the teachers requested; and the objection of some individual or group in the community to the presence in the school library of books considered to be "potentially dangerous" to the minds of students.

## Book Selection or Censorship?

The first problem is probably more complex and difficult than the second, because a convincing distinction cannot always be made between "book selection," which is considered to be a good and necessary operation, and "censorship," which is considered to be bad. The librarian never has enough dollars to come even close to buying as many books as are needed. Consequently she tries to buy only the best books available. To determine what is "best," she uses standard lists, book reviews, bibliographies, and direct guidance by experts. This is book selection. But sometimes the book in question may be a good book and yet one which, in the judgment of the administrators, or the librarian, might be offensive to people in the community—and not necessarily the cranks or crackpots. Salinger's *Catcher in the Rye* has frequently been involved in this kind of controversy.

It would seem that there is no single, clear-cut way of meeting the problem. If a teacher wishes to have her students read a particular book, her request should be honored—except in those rare cases when she shows an obvious lack of common sense in her selection of materials. For example, if a high school teacher assigned *Fanny Hill* as a book students were to read to learn about the attitude of men toward women in the seventeenth century, she would be using poor judgment. On the other hand, if she assigned *Catcher in the Rye* to help students understand the reactions of youth to their problems in their own time, she would be using good judgment. The judgment required to distinguish between these two cases is formed by a knowledge of history and literature, an understanding of the needs and capacities of youth, and some understanding of the temper of the community. At the same time, one must know which books are available for purchase in the bookstores. The difference between book selection and censorship is obviously not clear-cut; a librarian or superintendent may be practicing censorship under the guise of book selection.

The problem of labeling concerns books already in the library. There are certain to be individuals and groups in the community who will admit the necessity of having a specific book in the library, provided it is labeled so that the reader can be warned of the danger the individual or the group thinks the book contains. This pressure should be resisted flatly and without compromise, for the clear reason that what is "liberal" to one person may be "conservative" to another. Students must be allowed to build up their own immunity against falsehood, by constant exposure to all kinds of evidence. One might say that the "shots" one can take to prevent being taken in by falsehoods are found in the teaching program of the school. If, for instance, a student cannot tell from the contents of a book that it is Communist propaganda, then obviously the student has no immunity. This he can get by being taught what Communism is. Then the student would be able to identify the nature of whatever he was reading and labels would be unnecessary.

## Dealing with Censorship

Censorship, when it arises from some individual or group in the community, is relatively easier to handle. If the librarian has been careful to ascertain the quality of the materials added to the library or their appropriateness to a specific teaching activity, then, on the basis of the principles stated earlier in the American Library Association Bill of Rights, pressure for removal of the book from the school library can and should be resisted vigorously. A school library is not a university library, and cannot justify the presence of books on its shelf that would legitimately be found in a university library. The books should be selected for their quality and for their appropriateness to specific teaching needs. The two criteria cannot always be separated. One can, for example, assume that university libraries collected volumes of *Eros* as relevant source material for the study of pornography as an aspect of abnormal psychological behavior, but this title would likely not be appropriate for a school library unless it were ordered by a faculty member who, with the consent of the administration, attempted to teach students about pornography and who wished to use a copy of *Eros* to illustrate a point. In such a case the instructor would want to make certain the administration knew, in advance, that she intended to teach a subject that might be misunderstood by the public. Taste and judgment are involved in such questions. For instance, every high school student presumably needs to be aware of the institution of prostitution, but it might not be a good idea to bring a madam to class to illustrate the point.

Censorship has come and gone in the United States. Since the war, ultraconservatives have attempted to remove from school libraries books they think might influence students toward Communism. But in their zeal, they would take out books that qualified scholars would select as accurate, scholarly, and useful books necessary to an understanding of the social studies. These efforts have to be resisted on principle.

Fortunately, there are other kinds of community relations that can be positive in nature. For example, the school library could be usefully enriched if citizens became interested in hunting up some material about the community that could be used in various departments of the school. Books written by famous people who once lived in the community, and printed evidence of the progress of business and agricultural and industrial firms in the area could be collected. Special endowment funds might be raised to permit the buying of books in special fields for which there is not enough money in the budget—travel books, for instance. The buying of such books would be coordinated with the other work of the library.

# CHAPTER IX

# Experimentation: Standards Versus Goals

Schools have had some difficulty in convincing the public of the value of something for which no existing examples can be found. This has been true of school libraries. The Knapp Foundation made a $1.3 million grant in 1961, to be administered by the American Association of School Librarians to establish demonstrations of what good school library service can mean. The first phase involved two demonstrations, one in the Central Park Road Elementary School in Plainsville, New York, the other in the Marcus Whitman Elementary School in Richland, Washington. Two other demonstrations were planned for 1964 and three in secondary schools for 1965. Since the demand for good school library service was so clearly realized during this period, the influence of these demonstration centers was expected to be widespread.

## Standards Versus Goals

This volume could be considered as a statement of those goals which the good school library might be expected to achieve. Statements of standards, such as the one published by the American Library Association, attempt to state in terms of quantifications and specific procedures what is essential to the achievement of these goals, but statements of standards may not necessarily represent good statements of the goals the standards are supposed to support. Thus a school administrator eager to have a good school library might meet the Association's standards and still not have a library that would accomplish the goals he had in mind. Statements of goals and statements of standards supplement each other. Neither is very useful without the other.

It was in the statement and description of goals that the literature of school librarianship was weakest at a crucial moment—the 1960's —when school administrators were eager to take a major step forward in improving their school libraries. The school library profession, for reasons that were predictable to anyone who had studied conditions in school libraries in the past, had developed few spokesmen who could produce programs capable of winning the admiration of the most enlightened school administrators and the support of the public. For example, the Educational Facilities Laboratories, Inc., called a conference in June 1964 to bring leading school librarians and a few recognized school administrators together to consider what could be done to improve elementary school libraries. An impartial observer reported to the author that the librarians had less to offer that was fresh and interesting than did some of the administrators, who had obviously been thinking about the problem in new and interesting ways and were articulate in describing their ideas.

Most librarians in this period readily conceded that the profession had been unable, because of low salary levels and unfavorable working conditions, to attract to its ranks large numbers of outstandingly articulate people. But, at the same time, there were many school librarians who wanted to do the very things the administrators were able to discuss, even though they may not have been able to verbalize their hopes.

School librarians were puzzled and hurt when good statements of standards, such as the Association of School Libraries' *Standards for School Library Programs*,[1] were not accepted by administrators and others as sound statements of goals. The librarians assumed that everyone understood their goals and that it was not necessary to talk about them.

To some extent, their point of view was shared by public, college, and university librarians in this period. In discussing the importance of libraries among themselves, they would talk, not about what they wanted to be doing, but about the obstacles that prevented them from realizing their goals. For example, a university librarian might have considerable difficulty in justifying to an appropriations committee of a state legislature her need for a two-million-volume library, not because she didn't know why the books were needed but because she assumed the legislators should not have to have so obvious a matter explained to them. Or, to cite another example, any

---

[1] American Association of School Libraries, *Standards for School Library Programs* (Chicago: American Library Association, 1960).

good college reference librarian who has spent hours teaching a student how to use the bibliographical tools he must master before he
can find the information he needs to write a paper, may be doing an
excellent job, but when asked to explain why she thinks her work
should be called teaching or why she should be given a faculty title
or an academic rank, she is likely to be unable to generalize her
account of her own activities sufficiently to convince others. Her
reaction is likely to be: "Why shouldn't this be self-evident?"

For this reason, the best statements of library goals were frequently made by outsiders. For example, Harvie Branscomb's
*Teaching with Books*,[2] still stands as one of the best statements of
what a college library should be doing. This contrasts with Guy
Lyle's *The Administration of a College Library*,[3] which is an excellent statement of how a college library should operate.

Francis Henne's "Toward Excellence"[4] represents a good, con-
cise statement of school library goals. Many of the speeches J.
Lloyd Trump made at library meetings during 1962 and 1963 were
of a similar quality and nature. These stand out among the hundred
of journal articles written by school librarians about how they do
their work, many of which were useful to the practicing librarian
but few of which helped to increase the administrators' understanding of why school libraries were essential to the school program.

Unfortunately, because of their inarticulateness, school librarians
were not given credit for the many interesting, important, and creative dreams of fine library service some of them had.

---

2 Harvie Branscomb, *Teaching with Books* (Chicago: American Library Association, 1931).

3 Frances B. Keppel, reported in *St. Louis Post-Dispatch*, June 1964.

4 Francis Henne, "Toward Excellence," *Library Quarterly* (January 1960),
75–90.

# CHAPTER X

# A Forecast: The Immediate Future

The preceding chapters have attempted to summarize the most significant developments in the various aspects of the school library field. But because these developments were slow and meager prior to the 1950's, and because almost no satisfactory research on school library problems had been done, much attention has been given to the new ideas, plans, and programs that were shaping up at the time of this writing.

This chapter will re-examine some of these new developments so that they can be seen as a statement of goals for school libraries in the second half of the twentieth century.

### School Libraries: An Essential Part
### of the Modern School

Even as late as 1964, many secondary schools and most elementary schools were without satisfactory school libraries. Francis B. Keppel, U.S. Commissioner of Education, speaking at a meeting in St. Louis, Missouri, in June 1964, said, "It is a national disgrace that 60 per cent of American schools, with ten million of America's children, have no school libraries whatsoever."[1] He also commented that "the evidence is incontrovertible that the ability to learn and study goes hand in hand with the ability to earn and to succeed in our modern society. . . . A school without a library is a crippled school."

The first tangible evidence of the librarians' realization that they would have to stop blaming school administrators for these conditions and assume responsibility themselves for major breakthroughs, was the conference-within-a-conference held at the annual conference of the American Library Association in Chicago in June 1963. This was precipitated by the fact that an explosive demand for li-

---

[1] Frances B. Keppel, reported in *St. Louis Post-Dispatch*, June 1964.

brary service by schoolchildren had spilled over into public and college libraries. Librarians realized for the first time that a new and more comprehensive community-wide solution to the problem of school library service had to be found—and quickly.

Publication of *The School Library* (1963) by Educational Facilities Laboratories, Inc., in which it was stated that a secondary school library has to have a minimum of 30,000 volumes in cities where other good libraries are available to students, and 50,000 volumes in cities where other libraries do not exist, focused attention on the critical nature of the problem.

Fortunately, there were a few examples that served as pacesetters. As examples of aggressive and forward-looking school library supervisors in city and state education departments, one could cite Miss Cora Bomar in North Carolina; Paul Reed in Rochester, N.Y.; Eleanor Alexander in Houston, Texas; and Frances Hatfield in Broward County, Florida. Enlightened administrators such as Arno de Bernardis in Portland, Oregon, Harry Koss in Naperville, Illinois, and Harry Moore in Littleton, Colorado—to cite only a very few—gave strong support to the cause of better school libraries. Academics such as Paul Witty at Teachers College, Columbia University, J. Lloyd Trump at the University of Illinois, Stephen Romine at the University of Colorado, Miss Mary Gaver at Rutgers University, Frances Henne at Columbia University, and Louis Shores at Florida State University helped lay an intellectual base for practical programs.

The essential question in the early 1960's was no longer whether a school library was essential, but rather how to finance and staff it and how to find enough space for it.

## Working Relations Between School Librarians and School Administrators

As stated before, school librarians acquired enough self-confidence as well as competence to express their dissatisfaction with existing school libraries—not by talking among themselves, but by talking with administrators in terms of existing demonstrations of good school library service and in terms of educational concepts that included school library service as an essential part. Attention given to the problem by the Knapp Foundation demonstrations, and by publications of the Educational Facilities Laboratories, Inc., helped administrators who were looking for backing for their own desires to improve school libraries. Encouragement was also given by school architects, who quickly responded to the need for high-quality physical environments for learning.

### The Materials Center Movement

At its worst, the materials center movement was little more than a cheap jargonistic phrase to describe a relationship between printed books and other types of learning materials—especially the audio-visuals—in the school library. But at its best, it became a rallying cry for those librarians and media specialists who tried very hard to make it easy for faculty and students to use all the kinds of car-riers for knowledge in one place, under a single bibliographic con-trol, and under the guidance of librarians who were capable of knowing which carrier was most appropriate to a specific problem.

The specific kinds of carriers involved were printed books, jour-nals, newspapers, and pamphlets; motion picture films, slides, and filmstrips; art prints and art objects; tapes for programmed in-struction devices and for teaching machines; graphics; exhibits and displays; dioramas, phonograph records and tapes; microfilms, mi-crocards, and microfiche, and kinescopes and types of radio and television programs.

The special devices involved were microreading machines; pro-jectors of various kinds; record players and tape-recorders with ear-phones; teaching machines; television and radio receivers; and lis-tening posts at which more than one person could hear an aural program.

The special kinds of space requirements involved were assembly-ing rooms near the library office in which librarians, media special-ists, and teachers could work together to evaluate materials and to plan reading assignments and library acquisitions; inclusive study stations—the first of which, the Cornberg carrel, appeared in 1963; projection rooms for individual and small-group viewing of films; reading areas that could be darkened somewhat for the use of in-dividual filmstrip injectors and television reception; and staff offices.

There were new personnel requirements for librarians and audio-visual experts who understood each other's methods and materials and who could and would work as a team to provide an enriched body of teaching and learning materials in the library as well as in the classrooms, laboratories, and studios.

A materials center library required considerably more space than one that contained only printed books, and the cost of the space was greater because of the requirements for access to electrical power and to transmission cables as well as because of the requirements for soundproofing.

One new machine system that had important implications for school libraries was in the process of development in late 1964. This was a variant of the existing Xerox-TDX transmitter that would transmit directly the image of a book or periodical page, via cables, from one part of a building or a campus to another. This would be, in effect, a system based on splitting a Xerox-914 copier in two, with the sender in the library and various receivers in other parts of the school. It was expected that this device would be in operation in 1965. The images would be carried over a TDX cable containing from twenty to sixty wires. A conduit, some four inches in diameter, would be required.

A school owning this system would be able to transmit, to various parts of the school, pages from books or periodicals upon request, thus opening up new possibilities for the use of reference material— material that is in heavy demand in the school library. It is expected that the largest part of the cost of this system will be in the cables. It is not known at the time of this writing whether these would be rented from the telephone company or purchased outright by the school. A safe assumption is that this system would be as revolutionary in the secondary school library as the Xerox-914 copier has been in college and university libraries.

## The Team-Teaching Idea

Properly conceived, the team-teaching plan offers one answer to many of the frustrations librarians have never been able to overcome; improperly conceived, the plan could be a degrading curse to librarians.

Basically, the plan involves making a careful analysis of each operation in the teaching process and assigning each operation to an individual qualified to deal with it. This contrasts with the traditional plan which requires one teacher to do everything—from taking the roll, grading papers, and selecting books for the library to studying, lecturing, and teaching. The team-teaching plan assumes that in most communities there will be men and women—"resource people" as the jargon has it—who can spend a little time doing a specific operation in the teaching program.

If the librarian and media specialists are used as co-equals with the teacher in planning an enriched assignment schedule, and if the librarian—as well as the teacher—can be given assistants to do work of lesser complexity, the plan works well. But when it is set up so that the librarians and media specialists are merely secondary bookchasers, having no part in the planning of the courses, and when the librarian is given no staff to relieve her of routine operations, then the plan does not accomplish much.

### Photo Reproduction and Miniaturization

Although seldom used in the schools, a very large volume of printed materials has been made available since 1930 in the form of microfilms, microcards, microprints, and microfiche, and any school that wants to build up its resources for study may purchase many books, periodicals, government documents, and newspapers in this form. Publishers offer specific titles and series of publications (for example, the University Microfilms, Inc., American culture series, American periodicals series, and American studies series; the "Lost Cause" microcard series, books listed in the Wagner Bibliograph on western travel; the Albert Boni series on French drama; the United Nations publications; and many others). Files of journals can be purchased in any one of the above microforms. Free, up-to-date catalogs of the titles offered by each of the main publishers are also available.

One new process—miniprint—is a product of one of the most fertile minds in the library profession, Dr. Ralph Shaw. The process, which came into existence in 1964, has important implications for school libraries. This is a printing process using low-reduction ratios. Pages of print, each about one-and-a-half by two inches in size, are photographed in rows on sheets. The sheets are then bound together into six-by-nine pamphlets one eighth of an inch thick. The cost comes to about one cent for five pages of print. The microprint publishers expect to begin by selling files of ten-year runs of fifty journals listed in the *Reader's Guide to Periodical Literature* and will then offer many books that school libraries need but cannot buy because they are out of print. The publishers will pay royalties and will respect copyright laws.

As described by Dr. Shaw, the process is not good for materials in which pictures are of the essence—e.g., *Life, Look, National Geographic*—or which are subject to high-density use. Because the microprints have to be read through a small, box-like reading machine, and because a given school might not be able to afford many such machines, congestion would occur if the school tried to make high-density-use material available in this form.

Nevertheless, this would appear to be an ideal way of acquiring a large number of the books and journals schools needed to support honors programs and independent-study programs, in which students are encouraged to write papers. The prints could also be used to provide a way for students to trace pictures from books instead of cutting them out of books or tracing them directly from book pages.

Because this process is in its early stages of development, school librarians will need to watch it closely. A descriptive brochure and other information can be obtained from Mr. Albert Daub, President, The Scarecrow Press, 257 Park Avenue South, New York, N.Y.

## Automation and Information Retrieval

Although anything written now on these subjects may be out of date before it gets into print, a brief summary of the state of the art at this time would seem appropriate.

Automation of certain library operations—order records, serials records, card catalog reproduction, and circulation records—are desirable. Care should be taken to use a system appropriate for the complexity and size of the operations. For example, most school libraries would find a machine punched-card system too elaborate and too expensive, whereas a McBee Keysort punched-card system would be appropriate for even a small school. A small school that could not afford one of the card catalog reproduction machines would probably purchase its books already catalogued, with sets of cards ready for filing.

*Information retrieval* is a term that is used loosely to cover all electronic systems for selecting, recording, describing, and transmitting information. It had little practical application in a school library system as of 1964, in spite of the fact that popularizers had written glowing descriptions of elementary school readers sitting at Cornberg carrels, pushing buttons and commanding the information now locked up in the great libraries of the world. This is not feasible because of the cost, because of the lack of hardware, because the information has not yet been put on tapes, and for other reasons, including copyright laws. Since the major part of the cost of the process consists of analyzing the literature and reducing it to transferable terminology, it is not likely that many schools will be able to afford to originate much information-supplying in their own laboratories. If a national plan for putting all available information on computer tapes is established, a student could, in theory, command it in his Cornberg carrel. Today the cost factor alone would make this impossible. If the national plan provides for the selling of copies of tapes—either from tape units or from computers—the larger schools, or possibly the central library in a large city, could afford to purchase some of them. The problem is far more complicated than it appears to be at first glance and careful studies would need to be made before a school invests any money in the idea. For example, it is completely understandable that in the excitement over the idea of a complete system of information retrieval, one might overlook the flexibility, the usefulness, and the economy of an older machine—the printed book. Reference books, especially in the hands of an experienced reference librarian, can be made to yield information very efficiently and economically. If the contents of the *Encyclopedia Britannica* were on computer tapes and had to be used through the consoles, to find the answer to a simple question like, "How many wives did Henry VIII have?" would require at least a half-hour's time (if the computer were free when the reader wanted his answer) and would cost from $60 to $120. Contrast this with the ease of going to a shelf and using the volumes in the school library.

It should also be remembered that it would also not necessarily be in the best interests of the student to be able to command all the information he needed without any effort on his part. An essential element in the process of self-education at the elementary and secondary levels is the ability to learn how to learn—a process that seems to be inevitably tied to the use of the contents of the carriers of knowledge. In other words, one learns history by working with the facts of history. It's the "working with" that is relevant. Even a mature scholar in history could not do all his research from the information he could get from a computer, even though he would find the computer useful, and even essential, in certain kinds of historical research.

## Programmed Teaching

Without getting involved with the Skinner-Pressey controversy over the relevance or value of programmed instruction and without failing to note that many phony teaching machines and tapes were put on the market in the first years after the idea was introduced, it should be fairly obvious that the idea has merit if properly used. It works. The printed book itself is a very sophisticated teaching machine, one that can be used without a power source and with ambient light! Every museum in the world is a living testimony to the value of programmed teaching. A successful diorama in a natural history museum is prepared with as much thought and care as most authors lavish on each chapter in their books.

The problem in the schools and colleges is not *if* but *how* and *when*. As long as libraries were thought of as places where books only were to be used, there was little opportunity to focus *all* the kinds of learning materials on the subjects that were being taught. This is why the phrase *materials center* is being used to describe what a modern school library should be like. One would expect that the school library of the future would look something like a combination of a library, a museum, an art gallery, a chemistry laboratory, and even a computer shop. And such a library will have to be managed by people who are far more than mere technicians skilled in books, audiovisual materials, or museum science.

## Independent Study and the Honors Plan

Although these two ideas were just beginning to become popular topics of conversation among schoolmen at the time this volume was written, it was clear that they would play a dominant role in shaping secondary education for many years. And it was equally clear that they would have as much effect on the way and extent to which school libraries would be used as they had in the colleges that had had long experience with them.

There is one aspect of the honors plan that deserves further discussion because if it is not clearly understood and carefully evaluated in terms of the difference between secondary schools and colleges, it could cause difficulty. The difference between departmental and general honors programs in colleges and schools is great. Recognition for high achievement in students' undergraduate major work has been traditional in the American college. But recognition for a special kind of intellectual power that students achieve, not by concentration on one narrow subject, but by crossing departmental lines and in a special kind of seminar in which the students carry on the discussion under the guidance of the faculty, is relatively new. The current popularity of the general honors program lies in this interdisciplinary freedom, coming at a time when so much of the research in a university seems to require a hyphenated approach involving several of the traditional departments or disciplines. Or, to put it another way, the general honors programs are a kind of an undergraduate expression of the same force that has created the new kinds of research probes.

But does it follow that this relationship carries down into the secondary school in the same way? One could agree that at that level students (at least those intending to follow academic curriculums in college) should be concerned with mastery of the fundamentals of each standard discipline and that time spent on consideration of interrelationships would weaken the preparation in fundamentals and would therefore be harmful. One could also agree that the high-school age level is not a time for evaluation. But, on the other hand, one could say that these claims are simply an expression of an older and inadequate psychology of learning and that what is good for the college level is also good for the high schools.

Any school considering the adoption of a general honors plan would certainly want to be very clear as to how it stood on this issue.

For the school library the evidence suggests that at the college level, other things being equal, the general honors plan generates a larger volume of reading than do the traditional departmental honors programs. But beyond that and of far greater relevance, it is the independent-study idea, which is involved in both plans, that makes the major difference. As stated before, it is axiomatic that in the class system combining formal class presentations with textbooks and reading assignments most students can get by with very little further use of the library. But when each student is allowed to set his own pace and is encouraged to find his own way of approaching a subject, it has been inevitable that he will rely more heavily on the standard tools of the literature of scholarship—reference books and bibliographies—because these have been developed as bridges between the individual inquirer and the literature itself.

Any fair-minded observer of the American education scene at all levels would have to admit the need to keep an open mind on the question of breadth *versus* depth in terms of success at the college level. But there would be little doubt that the students who have learned how to organize an attack on a problem and how to assemble and evaluate evidence—primary source material—will move about easily in the world of scholarship. And the independent-study plan, if the school has a good library to serve as the plan's laboratory, does encourage that kind of learning.

### Changing Mores and the Problems of Censorship

In Chapter VIII, the problem of censorship was discussed briefly as a point-of-view problem in community relations. In this section, it will be presented as a procedural problem, with a little attention to current sources of trouble.

Man has always had a hard time remembering that customs and mores change, but that the significance of these changes is not usually great. The flappers of the Jazz Age eventually married and, as middle-aged women, were no less responsible than their predecessors were or the sex-pots of today will be in their time. The hobble-skirted girls of the pre-World War I days presented interesting problems when trying to get into a buggy or a high-fendered car, but no more so than the tight-sheathed girl of 1964 getting into or out of a sports car. No discernible new consequences are apparent.

But without doubt the citizen of the 1960's has to face more worrying problems of all kinds and sizes than has any other generation. And it is not surprising that he is touchy about factors that appear to subvert values he prizes. Usually there are no objective or foolproof guidelines to help one evaluate the importance of the subversion. Because new ideas are frequently first expressed in books, it is inevitable that a worried man is likely to be on guard lest books, movies, and television programs subvert his children.

As a current example, take the question of how the problem of premarital sex is handled in novels, in movies, and in advertising. In the first place, there is no existing evidence that will offer parents or teen-agers any definitive answer to the question of whether, in the long run, it is good or bad in our kind of society to change this custom. We simply don't know—not even the parents who are likely to think they know. Contemporary novelists, movie writers and directors, and Madison Avenue policy-makers appear to have decided either that the custom should change or that they will portray the changes that have occurred. Few of them appear to be opposed to the change. Thus the novels, the movies, and the advertisements the teen-ager sees tend to look with favor upon premarital sex relations. Shall the high school librarian keep out of the library these novels or shall she buy the best of the new novels and run the risk of parental opposition?

Or, to illustrate the problem at a more complex level, take the question of the proper economic organization of the modern state— capitalism or socialism. Spokesmen for each point of view are equally sincere and equally certain that their system is better. But expert economists of either persuasion know that there is no real way of predicting what the current technological innovations will do to the nature of the economic organization. Shall the school librarian refrain from buying economics or political books that reflect theories or arguments that are not orthodox? If she does not refrain, there will be organized groups in the community that will put pressure on her to do so.

There are two basic attitudes or positions a school librarian can take on the problem illustrated by these issues. The first one, well-expressed in a paragraph taken from a speech given by Supreme Court Justice Leonard Hand before the Board of Regents, University of the State of New York, October 24, 1952, is that all appropriate evidence on all sides of questions that are within teaching programs of the school should be present in the school library.

That "community" is already in the process of dissolution where every man begins to eye his neighbor as a possible enemy, where noncomformity with the accepted creed, political as well as religious, is a mask of disaffection; where denunciation, without specification or backing; takes the place of evidence; where orthodoxy chokes the freedom of dissent; where faith in the eventual supremacy of reason has become so timid that we dare not enter our convictions in the open lists, to win or lose.[1]

The second attitude is that exposure is potentially dangerous and that people—young and old—must be allowed to read only those books that the state considers safe. It is the position taken by the political extremists, on both the Left and the Right. In Europe, for instance, the extremists in Nazi Germany, Fascist Italy, Soviet Russia, and Franco Spain saw to it that the people were allowed to read only those books the government believed to be good for the people.

In this country, the extremists on the Right exert much pressure on the school libraries (see files of the American Library Association's *Newsletter on Intellectual Freedom*) to remove books which contain expressions of dissent, on the assumption that high school youths are likely to be drawn to doctrines that are evil, as the parents see them.

School librarians and administrators cannot escape or straddle this problem. They must accept the position favored by Supreme Court Justice Hand if they intend to remain in the American tradition. The only option left to them consists of using the skill with which they deal with problems at all levels—local, state, and national—when attacks are made on them. That there are many occasions for the exercise of this skill can be demonstrated by an examination of the cases reported in the American Library Association's monthly "Newsletter on Intellectual Freedom."[2] Eric Moon's article, "Problem Fiction," in *Library Journal*[3] proves conclusively that some school and public librarians are practicing censorship under the guise of book selection.

Two statements are reprinted as guides to proper procedures when problems of censorship arise. Both statements have been carefully worked out by thoughtful people who have been involved with the problem. The first one deals with selection—"preventive censorship."

[1] Judge Learned Hand, reported in *The New York Times,* October 25, 1952.
[2] "Newsletter on Intellectual Freedom." Published by the American Library Association, Chicago, Ill.
[3] Eric Moon, "Problem Fiction," *Library Journal* (1962).

I. *Policies and Procedures for Selection of School Library Materials*[4]

The following statement of policy-making with regard to materials selection for school libraries is offered as a guide to those wishing to formulate a policy. It is believed that such a policy should be formally adopted by each school district as a basis for consistent excellence in choice of materials and as a document that can be presented to parents and other citizens for their further understanding of the purposes and standards of selection of school library materials.

*Patterns of Policy-Making:*

The governing body of a school is legally responsible for all matters relating to the operation of that school. It is recommended that the assumption of responsibility and the delegation of authority be stated in a formal policy adopted by the legally responsible body.

*Selection Personnel:*

Materials for school libraries should be selected by professional personnel in consultation with administration, faculty, students, and parents. Final decision on purchase should rest with professional personnel in accordance with the formally adopted policy.

*Types of Materials Covered:*

There should be criteria established for all types of materials included in a library collection. Such criteria should be available in written form.

*Objectives of Selection:*

The primary objective of a school library is to implement, enrich, and support the educational program of the school. Other objectives are concerned with: (1) the development of reading skill, literary taste, discrimination in choice of materials, and (2) instruction in the use of books and libraries.

The school library should contribute to development of the social, intellectual, and spiritual values of the students.

*Criteria for Selection:*

1. Needs of the individual school:
   A. Based on knowledge of the curriculum;
   B. Based on requests from administrators and teachers.
2. Needs of the individual student:
   A. Based on knowledge of children and youth;
   B. Based on requests of parents and students.

---

[4] This has been approved by the Board of the American Association of School Librarians at the American Library Association Midwinter Conference, February 3, 1961, and published by the California Library Association.

3. Provision of a wide range of materials on all levels of difficulty, with a diversity of appeal and the presentation of different points of view.
4. Provision of materials of high artistic quality.
5. Provision of materials with superior format.

*Selection Tools:*

Reputable, unbiased, professionally prepared selection aids should be consulted as guides.

*Challenged Materials:*

A procedure should be established for consideration of and action on criticism of materials by individuals or groups. The School Library Bill of Rights, endorsed by the Council of the American Library Association in July 1955, is basic to this procedure.[5]

*Examples of Policy Statements:*
*School Library Association of California Bulletin*

*The Value of a Statement of Policy and Procedure:*

There are many reasons why a school district should have a written statement detailing a clearly defined procedure for the selection of library materials.

1. A written statement will make it easier for all school personnel—teachers, librarian, principals, supervisors, superintendents, and members of the governing board—to be fully informed on the specific book-selection practices of the district.

2. The responsibilities of participating individuals and the limits of their responsibilities will be explicitly stated.

3. If criteria are clearly detailed, and techniques for applying them are clearly set forth, those persons responsible for doing the actual selection will do a thorough and efficient job. Written criteria will serve as a basis for common agreement for those responsible for the selection of material.

4. The materials selected by such criteria and procedures will be better and more useful.

5. A written statement of policies and procedures is an aid in keeping the community informed on the selection of library materials. The confidence of the community in its schools will be increased by the knowledge of the thorough and reasoned philosophies and procedures underlying the selection of materials for its school libraries.

---

[5] "The Library Bill of Rights," *American Library Association Bulletin* (November 1953), 485.

*Suggested Contents for a Statement of Book-Selection Policy:*

On the local level, a statement of book-selection policy should include:

1. A statement of the philosophy of book selection for school libraries such as is given in the School Library Bill of Rights of the American Association of School Librarians, or the Book Selection Policy (Tentative) of the School Library Association of California, Northern Section.

2. A statement that the governing board of the district is legally responsible for the selection of library materials.

3. A statement detailing the delegation of this responsibility to professionally trained personnel.

4. An outline of the procedures and criteria to be applied throughout the school or district in selecting library materials.

5. A routine procedure for handling library materials that may be questioned by individuals or groups within the community.

*Policy on Selection of Materials for School Libraries:*

(Developed by a [Florida] County Organization of School Librarians)

We, as a group, are in accord with the policy of the National Education Association's Commission to Defend Democracy Through Education, which is to encourage young people to locate, use, and evaluate relevant materials of instruction as they identify and analyze significant contemporary problems and form judgments about them. However, it is not our duty to direct or compel any particular judgments. We do feel that it is a basic duty of the school library to make available materials of sound literary quality and authority presenting the history of American democracy and its underlying principles.

In formulating our policy, we considered these subjects which have been topics of criticism: religion, ideologies, sex, and science.

1. *Religion.* Factual, unbiased material which represents all major religions should be included in the library collection.

2. *Ideologies.* The library should, without making any effort to sway reader judgment, make available basic factual information on the level of its reading public, on any ideology or philosophy which exerts a strong force, either favorable or unfavorable, in government, current events, politics, education, or any other phase of life.

3. *Sex and Profanity.* Materials presenting accents on sex should be subjected to a stern test of literary merit and reality by the librarian, who takes into consideration her reading public. While we would not in any case include the sensational or overdramatic, the fact of sexual incidents or profanity appearing should not automatically disqualify a book. Rather, the decision should be made on

the basis of whether the book presents life in its true proportions, whether circumstances are realistically dealt with, and whether the book is of literary value. Factual material of an educational nature on the level of the reader public should be included in the library collection.

4. *Science.* Medical and scientific knowledge should be made available without any biased selection of facts.

*Basic Principles for the Selection of Materials for the East Greenbush Central School District School Libraries Adopted at a meeting of the Board of Education March 22, 1954*

It is the policy of the East Greenbush Central School District to select materials for our libraries in accordance with the following:

1. Books and other reading matter shall be chosen for values of interest and enlightenment of all the students of the community. A book shall not be excluded because of the race, nationality, or the political or religious views of the writer.

2. There shall be the fullest practical provision of material presenting all points of view concerning the problems and issues of our times, international, national, and local; and books or other reading matter of sound factual authority shall not be proscribed or removed from library shelves because of partisan or doctrinal disapproval.

3. Censorship of books shall be challenged in order to maintain the school's responsibility to provide information and enlightenment.

Interpreting these principles in selection of reading material more specifically, the following will apply:

1. We believe it is the right and responsibility of teachers and librarians to select reading material which is carefully balanced to include various points of view of any controversial subject.

2. Since materials are selected to provide for the interest and needs of the school community and the school program, therefore they will be selected cooperatively by teachers, principals, and librarians, sometimes with the assistance of students.

3. Selections of materials will be assisted by the reading, examination, and checking of standard evaluation aids; i.e., standard catalogues and book-review digests.

4. Two basic factors, truth and art, will be considered in the selection of books and other library materials. The first is factual accuracy, authoritativeness, balance, integrity. The second is a quality of stimulating presentation, imagination, vision, creativeness, style appropriate to the idea, vitality, distinction.

5. Materials for the school library shall be examined to select those in which the presentation and the subject matter are suitable for the grade and the interest level at which they are to be used.

They will be considered in relation both to the curriculum and to the personal interests of pupils and teachers.

Books and materials meeting the above standards and principles will not be banned but books or materials of an obscene nature or those advocating overthrow of the government of the United States by force or revolution shall not be recommended for purchase.

Criticisms of books that are in the library should be submitted in writing to the Superintendent. The Board of Education will be informed. Allegations thus submitted will be considered by a committee among the faculty which will be appointed by the Superintendent. This committee will be in the subject-matter field of the book or material challenged and the challenged book or material will be judged by the committee as to its conformity to the aforementioned principles. The books or materials involved will be suspended pending a decision in writing by the above committee. Appeals from this decision may be made through the Superintendent to the Board of Education for final decision.[6]

The second statement offers suggestions on how to avoid getting into trouble and what to do if a school is subjected to attacks.

## II. *How Libraries and Schools Can Resist Censorship*[7]

Libraries of all sizes and types have been under increasing pressures from persons who wish to use the library as an instrument of their own tastes and views. Such individuals and groups are demanding the exclusion or removal of books to which they object or the inclusion of a higher proportion of books that support their views. Similar attacks have been made on schools in connection with books used in their programs. In view of this fact, it seems desirable to set forth a few basic principles that may help librarians, trustees, and school administrators in preserving the freedom and professional integrity of their institutions.

The problem differs somewhat between the public library, with a responsibility to the public to present as wide a spectrum of significant reading matter as its budget can afford, and the school library, whose collections are designed to support the educational objectives of the school. In both, however, there is involved the freedom of

---

[6] Reprints included in California Library Association Packet on Intellectual Freedom, 1964.

[7] Adapted February 1, 1962, by the American Library Association Council and endorsed by the Adult Education Association of the U.S.A., Executive Committee; the American Book Publishers Council, the American Civil Liberties Union; the National Book Committee; the National Council of Teachers of English; the National Education Association Committee on Professional Rights and Responsibilities; and the National Education Association Department of Classroom Teachers.

the school or the library to meet its professional responsibilities to the whole community.

Every library or school should take certain measures to clarify its policies and establish its community relations. These steps should be taken without regard to any attack or prospect of attack. They will put the institution in a firm and clearly defined position if its book policies are ever called into question.

As a normal operating procedure, every library, and the administration responsible for it, should establish certain principles.

1. There should be a definite book-selection policy. This should be in written form and approved by the board of trustees, the school board, or other administrative authority. It should be stated clearly and should be understood by members of the staff. This policy should apply to other materials equally, i.e., films, records, magazines, and pamphlets.

2. A file recording the basis for decision should be kept for titles likely to be questioned or apt to be considered controversial.

3. There should be a clearly defined method for handling complaints. Any complaint should be required to be in writing, and the complainant should be identified properly before the complaint is considered. Action should be deferred until full consideration by appropriate administrative authority.

4. There should be continuing efforts to establish lines of communication to assure mutual understanding with civic, religious, educational, and political bodies.

5. Newspapers of the community should be informed of policies governing book selection and use. Purposes and services of the library should be interpreted through a continuing public relations program, as should the use of books in the school.

6. Participating in local civic organizations and in community affairs is desirable. The library and the school are key centers of the community; the librarian and school administrator should be known publicly as community leaders.

If an attack does come, remember the following:

1. Remain calm. Don't confuse noise with substance. Most attacks come from small groups of people who have little community backing. Time after time the American people have shown that, given the facts, they will back solidly the responsible exercise of professional freedom by teachers and librarians and that they will insist on protecting their own freedom to read. Insist on the deliberate handling of the complaint under previously established rules. Treat complainants with dignity, courtesy, and good humor.

2. Take immediate steps to assure that the full facts surrounding a complaint are known to the administration. The school librarian

should go through the principal to the superintendent and the school board; the public librarian, to the board of trustees or to the appropriate community administration official; the college or university librarian, to the president and through him to the board of trustees. Full, written information should be presented giving the nature of the problem or complaint and identifying the source.

3. Seek the support of the local press immediately. The freedom to read and the freedom of the press go hand in hand.

4. Inform civic (local) organizations of the facts and enlist their support where possible.

5. Defend the principles of the freedom to read and the professional responsibility of teachers and librarians rather than the individual book. The laws governing obscenity, subversive material, and other questionable matter are subject to interpretation by the courts. The responsibility for removal of any book from public access should rest with this established process. The responsibility for the use of books in the schools must rest with those responsible for the educational objectives being served.

6. The American Library Association Intellectual Freedom Committee and other appropriate national and state committees concerned with intellectual freedom should be informed of the nature of the problem. Even though such effort at censorship must be met at the local level, there is often value in the support and assistance of agencies outside the area which have no personal involvement. They often can cite similar or parallel cases and suggest methods of meeting an attack. Similar aid in cases affecting the use of books in the schools can be obtained from the Commission on Professional Rights and Responsibilities of the National Education Association.

Every librarian should be familiar with certain basic documents which have been prepared by the American Library Association and represent the position of this national organization of more than 26,000 librarians.[8]

---

[8] California Library Association Packet, *op. cit.*

# Bibliography

American Association for the Advancement of Science, *Report on Broad Improvements in Science Teaching.* New York: Science Education News, 1962.

American Association of School Libraries, *Standards for School Library Programs.* Chicago: American Library Association, 1960.

Beust, Nora E., *School Library Standards, 1954.* U.S. Office of Education Bulletin No. 15. Washington, D.C.: USGPO, 1954.

Branscomb, Harvie, *Teaching with Books.* Chicago: American Library Association, 1931.

Brown, J. W., R. B. Lewis, and F. F. Hardervood, *Instruction: Materials and Methods.* New York: McGraw-Hill Book Company, 1959.

Calvin, H. R. and K. Devereau, *Proceedings of the Library Buildings Institute,* St. Paul, Minn., June 1954. Chicago: American Library Association, 1955.

Cassierer, H. H., *Television Teaching Today.* Paris, France: UNESCO, 1961.

Chase, Francis and Harold A. Anderson, *High Schools in a New Era.* Chicago: The University of Chicago Press, 1958.

Chase, Francis, "America Evaluates Its Schools," *Library Quarterly* Vol. 30 (1960).

Conant, James B., *Education and Liberty.* Cambridge, Mass.: Harvard University Press, 1953.

Council of Chief State School Officers, *Purchase Guide for Programs in Science, Mathematics, and Modern Foreign Languages.* Boston: Ginn & Company, 1959.

Department of Audiovisual Education, "Film, the New Language." Boulder, Colo.: University of Colorado, 1962.

Dewey, John, *Interest and Effort in Education.* Boston: Houghton Mifflin Company, 1913.

Educational Facilities Laboratories, Inc., *Study Carrels: Designs for Individual Study Space.* Stanford: The School Planning Laboratory, Stanford University, 1962.

————. *Study Carrels—Designs for Independent Study Space.* Stanford: The School Planning Laboratory. Stanford University, 1963.

Ellsworth, Ralph E. and Hobart Wagener, *The School Library.* New York: Educational Facilities Laboratories, Inc., 1963.

Fargo, Lucille, *The Library in the School.* Chicago: American Library Association, 1947.

Gruber, H. E. and Morris Weitman, *Self-Directed Work Experiments in Higher Education.* University of Colorado Behavior Research Report 19. Boulder, Colo., April 1962.

Henne, Francis, "Toward Excellence," *Library Quarterly* (January 1960).

Illinois Library Association, *Planning the School Library Quarters.* Chicago: American Library Association, 1950.

Independent Schools Education Board, *Three Thousand books for Secondary School Libraries.* New York: R. R. Bowker Co., 1961.

Knapp, Patricia, "The Monteith Experiment," *College and Research Libraries* (July 1961).

"The Library Bill of Rights," *American Library Association Bulletin,* (November 1953).

*Library Literature,* ed. Dorothy Cole. New York: H. W. Wilson Co., 1921+.

Logan, Henry, "Lighting Libraries," *Library Journal* (1952).

Lohrer, Alice, "School Libraries as Instructional Materials Centers, with Implications for Training: A Progress Report of This Study Under Title VIII, National Defense Education Act."

Metcalf, Keyes D. "Lighting," in forthcoming book on college and university library buildings, to be published by McGraw-Hill Book Company in 1965.

————, *Light and Vision.* University of Michigan Continued Education Series No. 76. Ann Arbor: University of Michigan, 1958.

Moon, Eric, "Problem Fiction," *Library Journal* Vol. 87 (February 1962).

"Newsletter on Intellectual Freedom." Chicago: American Library Association, 1962.

Roseoff, Martin, *The Library in High School Teaching.* New York: H. W. Wilson Co., 1959.

Schofield, E. T., "Competencies Needed by School Librarians for Selecting and Organizing Materials for Materials Center," *The School Libraries as a Materials Center,* U.S. Office of Education Circular No. 708. Washington, D.C.: USGPO, 1963.

Shores, Louis, *Instructional Materials: An Introduction for Teachers.* New York: The Ronald Press Company, 1960.

Skinner, B. F., "Teaching Machines," *Scientific American* (November 1961).

Stolurow, L. M., *Teaching by Machines.* U.S. Office of Education. Cooperative Research Monograph, No. 6. Washington, D.C.: USGPO, 1961.

Stone, C. W., "The Crisis in Education—A Mandate for Libraries," *American Library Association Bulletin* (February 1961).

"Student Reactions to Study Facilities . . ." A Report to the Presidents of Amherst, Mount Holyoke, Smith College, and the University of Massachusetts. The Committee for the New College, Amherst, Mass., 1960.

Taylor, K. I., "Competencies Needed by School Librarians for Planning Quarters and Administrating the Use of Materials Center," *The School Libraries as a Materials Center,* U.S. Office of Education Circular No. 708. Washington, D.C.: USGPO, 1963.

Thompson, Anthony, *Library Buildings of Britain and Europe*. London: Butterworth & Co. (Publishers), Ltd., 1963.

Trinkner, Charles L., *Basic Books for Junior College Libraries: 20,000 Vital Titles*. Northport, Ala.: Colonial Press, 1963.

Trump, J. Lloyd, *Image of the Future*. Washington, D.C.: National Education Association, 1958.

————, *Images of the Future*. Washington, D.C.: National Education Association, 1959.

Walker, R. D., *The Availability of Library Service and Academic Achievement*, Research Series, No. 4. Chicago: Springfield, Illinois State Library, 1963.

Waples, Douglas and Ralph Tyler, *What People Want To Read About*, Chicago: The University of Chicago Press, 1931.

Wofford, A. M., *The School Library at Work*. New York: H. W. Wilson Co., 1959.

# Index

114